Child Abuse
Implications for
Child Development
and Psychopathology

David A. Wolfe

Volume 10, Second Edition
Developmental Clinical Psychology and Psychiatry

SAGE Publications
International Educational and Professional Publisher
Thousand Oaks   London   New Delhi

To Barb

SERIES EDITOR'S INTRODUCTION

Interest in child development and adjustment is by no means new. Yet only recently has the study of children benefited from advances in both clinical and scientific research. Advances in the social and biological sciences, the emergence of disciplines and subdisciplines that focus exclusively on childhood and adolescence, and greater appreciation of the impact of influences such as the family, peers, and school have helped accelerate research on developmental psychopathology. Apart from interest in the study of child development and adjustment for its own sake, the need to address clinical problems of adulthood naturally draws one to investigate precursors in childhood and adolescence.

Within a relatively brief period, the study of psychopathology among children and adolescents has proliferated considerably. Several different professional journals, annual book series, and handbooks devoted entirely to the study of children and adolescents and their adjustment document the proliferation of work in the field. Nevertheless, there is a paucity of resource material that presents information in an authoritative, systematic, and disseminable fashion. There is a need within the field to convey the latest developments and to represent different disciplines, approaches, and conceptual views to the topics of childhood and adolescent adjustment and maladjustment.

The Sage Series on **Developmental Clinical Psychology and Psychiatry** is designed to serve uniquely several needs of the field. The series encompasses individual monographs prepared by experts in the fields of clinical child psychology, child psychiatry, child development, and related disciplines. The primary focus is on developmental psychopathology, which refers broadly here to the diagnosis, assessment, treatment, and prevention of problems that arise in the period from infancy through adolescence. A working assumption of the series is that understanding, identifying, and important considerations in understanding the impact of child abuse on development and psychopathology (McGee & Wolfe, 1991; National Research Council, 1993).

Legal and Social Science Definitions

Legal statutes have attempted for more than three decades to define the minimal criteria acceptable for child care, with provisions for social or legal intervention specified under certain circumstances, such as nonaccidental injuries or inadequate medical attention. The general definition of child abuse that has emerged in conjunction with these statutes emphasizes the presence of nonaccidental injuries as a result of acts of commission (physical assault) or omission (failure to protect) by caretakers (Giovannoni & Becerra, 1979; Kempe & Helfer, 1972). Thus, statutorily defined physical abuse often refers most directly to a condition of physical harm to the child, but it also indirectly covers any child in need of protection—that is, a child whose life, health, or safety may be endangered by the conduct of his or her caregiver. Legal definitions are weighted heavily toward the overt consequences of abuse (e.g., bruises, welts, broken limbs), yet they serve an important purpose for delineating minimum community standards of child care. Civil legislation is considered to be a more child- and family-oriented approach to identifying and intervening in cases of suspected abuse, in contrast to criminal laws covering assault and related bodily offenses (Bross, 1997; Pamenter-Potvin, 1985), although criminal charges are often pursued in more serious cases of physical injury.

The legal-social definition of child abuse has shaped theory, research, and social intervention regarding all types of child maltreatment. This definition places a major emphasis on parental deviance and wrongdoing, thereby directing the focus predominantly on the implicit intent to inflict harm or on the incapability of the parent to protect the child from harm. However, the majority of physically abusive incidents (about 80%) involve minor injuries, typically occurring in the context of discipline (Herrenkohl, Herrenkohl, & Egolf, 1983; Kadushin & Martin, 1981), rather than major acts of assault. The definition has thus evolved to allow greater recognition of child abuse in its entire individual, family, and social context, including but not limited to adult deviance and purposeful intention to harm a child. Social scientists, for example, have considered the importance of social and familial variables, such as antecedents to abuse, the type of act committed, and the intensity of the reaction, that define child abuse within the context of child-rearing norms (Friedman, Sandler, Hernandez, & Wolfe, 1981; Giovannoni & Becerra, 1979).

Apart from the physical consequences of abuse, social scientists have focused on the developmental and psychological effects. The psychological impact of maltreatment is difficult to define, but it has the potential to harm the child in ways over and beyond the effects of physical injuries. Although a social-psychological definition often is not fully compatible with legal statutes and similar criteria outlining the global parameters of caregivers' rights and choices, such a definition is highly worthwhile for studying the impact of abuse on the child and the family.

A social-psychological perspective of child abuse places primary importance on the relationship context in which such events occur and have their greatest psychological impact. This emphasis derives from the fact that, in addition to physical injuries, child abuse represents a breakdown in the family's role as a facilitator of the child's social and cognitive development (Maccoby & Martin, 1983). Abuse is often enmeshed in other serious family problems, most notably parental substance abuse, financial problems, and stressful life circumstances, all of which are related to some degree to negative developmental outcomes. Therefore, the socialization practices that abusive and other distressed families have in common warrant consideration in defining the broader context of this problem.

Beyond legal and social science definitions, a straightforward description of child maltreatment can be obtained by considering the types of acts most commonly reported to child protective service agencies. The following descriptive definitions of the four principal types of maltreatment provide a practical understanding of terminology, incidence, and demographics based on empirically derived incident reports.

Child Protection Descriptions

Based on the above legal definitions, all states and provinces in North America have civil laws, or statutes, that obligate persons who come in contact with children as part of their job or volunteer work (bus drivers, day care workers, teachers, baby-sitters, and so forth) to report known or suspected cases of abuse to the police or child welfare authorities. These statutes also provide criteria for removing children from their homes who are suspected of being maltreated. Criminal statutes further specify the boundaries of permissible actions on the part of parents and parent surrogates, such as the use of corporal punishment to discipline children, as well as sanctions for violations. Typically, criminal charges are laid in more serious incidents of abuse or neglect, because the burden of proof in criminal matters can be difficult to achieve in cases of child abuse (i.e., a determination of guilt "beyond a reasonable doubt," as opposed to a finding of fact based on "the balance of probability" in civil matters, with no criminal penalty; Bross, 1997).

Child maltreatment is classified into four major types: physical abuse, child neglect, sexual abuse, and emotional abuse. The definition of each type has been refined on the basis of three National Incidence Studies (NIS) conducted by the U.S. Department of Health and Human Services in 1980, 1986, and 1993. NIS estimates are derived from official reports of abuse and neglect as well as a nationally representative sample of professionals who come in contact with maltreated children in a variety of settings. To account for the fact that maltreatment affects children regardless of actual physical injuries, the NIS definitions of maltreatment allow for two different sets of definitional standards: (a) the *harm standard,* whereby the child has suffered demonstrable harm as a result of maltreatment, such as a broken bone, and (b) the *endangerment standard,* which includes all of the harm standard children but adds in those whose maltreatment experiences put them in danger of being harmed, such as witnessing parental violence. Approximately three times as many children are endangered as harmed each year (Sedlak & Broadhurst, 1996).

Physical Abuse. Child physical abuse is the infliction or endangerment of physical injury as a result of punching, beating, kicking, biting, burning, shaking, or otherwise harming a child. The injuries are seldom intentional (the parent's heedless intention most often was to *control* the child), but nonetheless, the use of physical punishment and harsh disciplinary tactics can result in child injuries. The severity and nature of injuries resulting from physical abuse may range from minor (bruises, lacerations) to moderate (scars, abrasions) to severe (burns, sprains, or broken bones). Physical injuries represent only the visible scars of abuse, however. Chapter 3 describes how children's psychological development is often impaired in less visible, but very serious, ways as well. For example, due to harsh and insensitive treatment, physically abused children are often described as more disruptive and aggressive than other children their age and may show a wide range of emotional and cognitive problems (Aber & Cicchetti, 1984).

Neglect. Physical and emotional neglect are characterized by a failure to provide for children's basic physical, educational, or emotional needs. *Physical neglect* includes refusal of or delay in seeking health care, abandonment, expulsion from the home or refusal to allow a runaway to return home, and inadequate supervision. *Educational neglect* involves actions such as allowing chronic truancy, failure to enroll a child of mandatory school age in school, and failure to attend to a special educational need. *Emotional neglect* includes actions such as marked inattention to the child's needs for affection, refusal of or failure to provide needed psychological care, spousal abuse in the child's presence, and permission of drug or alcohol use by the child. The determination of child neglect requires consideration of cultural values and standards of care as well as recognition that the failure to provide the necessities of life is often embedded in poverty and social disadvantage.

Neglected children may suffer physical health problems, limited growth, and increased complications arising from other health conditions, such as diabetes and allergies. They may also show patterns of behavior that vacillate between undisciplined activity and extreme passivity (Crittenden & Ainsworth, 1989), because of their ways of adapting to an unresponsive caregiver. As toddlers, they show little persistence and enthusiasm, and as preschoolers, neglected children show poor impulse control and are highly dependent on teachers for support and nurturance (Erickson, Egeland, & Pianta, 1989). Emotional neglect includes children who witness domestic violence, experiences that may affect children in much the same ways as other forms of maltreatment. Such experiences have been linked to fear and distress in toddlers and preschoolers, including regressive and somatic signs of distress, such as sleep problems, bed-wetting, headaches, stomachaches, diarrhea, and ulcers. Among older children and adolescents, the impact of domestic violence has been linked to more aggression with peers and dating partners, as well as to lower self-esteem (McCloskey, Figueredo, & Koss, 1995; Wolfe, Jaffe, Wilson, & Zak, 1985).

Sexual Abuse. Sexual abuse includes fondling a child's genitals, intercourse, incest, rape, sodomy, exhibitionism, and commercial exploitation through prostitution or the production of pornographic materials. Sexual abuse may be underreported because of the secrecy or conspiracy of silence that so often characterizes these cases. The behavior and development of sexually abused children may be affected significantly, especially in relation to longer duration/greater frequency of abuse, the use of force, penetration, and a closer relationship to the perpetrator (Finkelhor & Browne, 1988; Kendall-Tackett, Williams, & Finkelhor, 1993). Their physical health may be compromised by urinary tract problems, gynecological problems, sexually transmitted diseases (including AIDS), and pregnancy (National Research Council, 1993). About one third of sexually abused children report or exhibit no visible symptoms, and about two thirds of those who

BOX 2.1

Child-Centered Methods

- Provides a variety of sensory stimulation and positive emotional expressions; engages in highly competent, child-centered inter-actions
- Communicates to children about normal sexuality and healthy relationships
- Makes rules for safety and health
- Occasionally scolds, criticizes, interrupts child activity; emotional delivery and tone sometimes harsh

Borderline Methods

- Shows rigid emotional expression and inflexibility in responding to child; uses verbal and nonverbal pressure to achieve unrealistic expectations
- Frequently uses verbal and nonverbal coercive methods and mini-mizes child's competence
- Is insensitive to child's needs
- Makes unfair comparisons
- Takes advantage of or ignores child's dependency status
- Impinges on the child's personal need for privacy

Inappropriate/Abusive/Neglectful Methods

- Denigrates, insults child
- Expresses conditional love and ambivalent feelings toward child
- Emotionally or physically rejects child's attention
- Uses cruel and harsh control methods
- Shows no sensitivity to child's needs
- Intentionally seeks out ways to frighten, threaten, or provoke child
- Responds unpredictably with emotional discharge
- Takes advantage of child's dependency status through coercion, threats, or bribes
- Is sexually or physically coercive and intrusive

SOURCE: Wolfe (1991). Used with permission.

emotional manner fall within the inappropriate and abusive range as does failure to respond to a child's needs, the cornerstone of neglect.

DETERMINANTS OF HEALTHY PARENT-CHILD RELATIONSHIPS

Having established a hypothetical range of acceptable and unacceptable child-rearing methods among North American families, it is also important to establish those features of a child's environment that should be fundamental and expectable (Scarr, 1992). Infants require protective and nurturant adults, as well as opportunities for socialization within a culture. Older children require things such as a supportive family, contact with peers, and ample opportunities to explore and master the environment as part of their expectable environment (Cicchetti & Lynch, 1995). Responsible parenting, moreover, involves a gradual shift of control from the parent to the child and the community. Seldom does this process go smoothly, yet healthy families are ones who learn to move gradually from nearly complete parental control, through shared control, to the child's growing self-control, into independence as an adult.

Determinants of healthy parent-child relationships and family roles from the perspective of optimal child development include the following: (Cicchetti & Lynch, 1995; Wekerle & Wolfe, 1993):

- Adequate knowledge of child development and expectations, including knowledge of children's normal sexual development and experimentation
- Adequate skill in coping with stress related to caring for small children and ways to enhance child development through proper stimulation and attention
- Opportunities to develop normal parent-child attachment and early patterns of communication
- Adequate parental knowledge of home management, including basic financial planning, proper shelter, and meal planning
- Opportunities and willingness to share the duties of child care between both parents, when applicable
- Provision of necessary social and health services

These healthy patterns depend, to a large extent, on interactions between the child, family, community, and cultural features. Child characteristics, such as temperament, health, and developmental abilities, interact with parental characteristics, such as competence and degree of developmental nonmaltreated disadvantaged children (Cicchetti & Rogosch, 1997). Thus, instead of thinking of maltreatment as a uniform stressor, these data demonstrate how the effects of maltreatment on development are dynamic and unpredictable. Regardless of whether or not a particular child shows demonstrable harm, however, does not detract from the fact that child maltreatment is harmful and poses significant risk to each child's development.

Abused children may be protected from harm if they have a positive relationship with at least one important and consistent person in their lives who provides support and protection (Kendall-Tackett, Williams, & Finkelhor, 1993; National Research Council, 1993). This person is typically the nonabusive parent or caregiver, but he or she could also be the identified parent, because from the child's point of view, a parent who at times yells, hits, and castigates may at other times be a source of connection, knowledge, or love (Wekerle & Wolfe, 1996). Paradoxically, it may be more adaptive for some children to focus on what their parents provide rather than on what they don't, because this permits them to see themselves as normal and accepted.

Similarly, a prime factor in how children respond to various forms of stress is the degree of support and assistance they receive from their parents to help them cope and adapt. Parents provide a model for the child that teaches them how to exert some control even in the midst of confusion and upheaval (Garmezy, 1983). A warm relationship with an adult who provides a predictable routine and consistent, moderate discipline and who buffers the child from unnecessary sources of stress is a valuable asset. Abused children may have the hardest time adapting appropriately to any form of stress to the extent that they are deprived of positive adult relationships, effective models of problem solving, and a sense of personal control or predictability (Hillson & Kuiper, 1994). This view has important implications for intervention efforts, because some interventions, such as removing children from their families, can become another source of stress and disruption that has undesired side effects (Melton, 1990).

The Psychological Significance of Child Maltreatment

Abused children experience ongoing, uncontrollable events that challenge their successful development and adaptation in a pervasive manner and that pose a threat to their core psychological well-being (Cicchetti & Lynch, 1995). They not only have to face acute and unpredictable parental outbursts or betrayal, they also have to adapt to environmental circumstances that pose developmental challenges. These influences include the more dramatic events, such as marital violence and separation of family members, as well as the mundane but important everyday activities that may be disturbing or upsetting, such as unfriendly interactions, few learning opportunities, and chaotic lifestyle. Because the source of stress and fear is centralized in their family, children who are maltreated are challenged on a regular basis to find ways to adapt that pose the least risk and offer maximum protection and opportunity for growth.

Child abuse and neglect have considerable psychological importance, because these experiences happen as part of ongoing relationships that are expected to be protective, supportive, and nurturing. Children from abusive and neglectful families grow up in an environment that fails to provide consistent and appropriate opportunities that guide development; instead, they are placed in jeopardy of physical and emotional harm (Wolfe & Jaffe, 1991). Yet their ties to their family—even to the abuser—are very important, so child victims may feel torn between a sense of loyalty and a sense of fear and apprehension. Because children depend on the people who harm or neglect them, they face other paradoxical dilemmas as well (American Psychological Association, 1996):

- *The child (victim) wants to stop the violence but also longs to belong to a family.* Loyalty and strong emotional ties to the abuser are powerful opponents to the victim's desire to be safe and protected.
- *Affection and attention may coexist with violence and abuse.* A recurring cycle may begin, whereby mounting tension characterized by fear and anticipation ultimately gives way to more abusive behavior. This may be followed by a period of reconciliation, with increased affection and attention. Children are always hopeful that the abuse will not recur.
- *The intensity of the violence tends to increase over time, although in some cases physical violence may decrease or even stop altogether.* Abusive behavior may vary throughout the relationship, taking verbal, sexual, emotional, or physical forms, but the adult's abuse of power and control remains the central issue.

As a result of increased recognition of these psychological effects, a significant shift is underway in how child maltreatment is defined and its effects are studied. As noted in Chapter 1, abuse was defined in the past primarily in terms of visible physical injuries. However, today we recognize that physical injuries are only one of many possible consequences. Maltreatment can also damage individuals' developing relations with others and their fundamental sense of safety and self-esteem.

new setting, Jimmy's pica disappeared and he seldom was difficult to manage by the foster parents. A fuller understanding of Jimmy's emotional disturbance then began to emerge within 3 weeks of placement in the foster home. He began to refer to his mother's boyfriend as a "bad guy" and described to the foster parents and social worker several abusive episodes in which the boyfriend had sprayed him in the face with a hose, kicked his ankle, flicked him in the eyes with his fingers, hit him on the head, and frightened him by putting him in the basement. The ensuing investigation confirmed that these episodes had occurred; his mother acknowledged that she had witnessed some of the abuse and eventually made her boyfriend leave the home. She explained that in her desperation to resolve some of Jimmy's earlier problems with bed-wetting and similar issues she had taken her boyfriend's advice and allowed Jimmy to be isolated from the family and mistreated.

Jimmy was eventually reunited with his mother, and reassessments of his development over several years indicated some continuity in terms of his interactions with his mother, peers, and teachers. Complaints from school described him as aggressive, pushing other children or hitting them with something. His first-grade teacher told the examiner "I'm never sure from one minute to the next how Jimmy will react to the other children. He could be playing and suddenly become angry at something and start to destroy things or hit someone. I've also seen him become frightened—at what I don't know—and withdraw into a corner. I've tried several times to discuss these things with his mother, but she says he's just trying to get his way all the time."

of child abuse seldom bear a linear relationship to child development, in that many individual, social, and environmental variables can modulate the impact of abuse on the child. Yet the trauma that almost invariably accompanies episodes of physical abuse and other forms of maltreatment can play a demonstrative role in affecting the child's ongoing adjustment and relationship formation.

Poor Relational Representation

Child maltreatment is known to disrupt the important process of attachment (Cicchetti, Toth, & Bush, 1988), a critical, ongoing process beginning between 6 and 12 months of age that normally provides infants with a secure, consistent base from which to explore and learn about their worlds. Episodes of child abuse and neglect, whether chronic or sporadic, can disrupt this natural process and interfere with children's ability to seek comfort and to regulate their own physiological and emotional processes. As a result, maltreated children are more likely than other children to show an absence of an organized attachment strategy (Cicchetti et al., 1988; Main & Solomon, 1990).

Both comparative and prospective studies support the conclusion that child abuse during infancy and early childhood is related to insecure attachment relationships with the caregiver (Dietrich, Starr, & Kaplan, 1980; Egeland & Sroufe, 1981; Egeland & Vaughn, 1981; Schneider-Rosen & Cicchetti, 1984). When observed in the strange situation, an unfamiliar task whereby the infant's behavior is studied in relation to the presence or absence of the mother, abused infants have been found to cling to their mothers and/or display negative affect toward their caregivers significantly more often than nonabused controls. Longitudinally, abused children who showed early attachment problems are more likely to reveal declining developmental abilities over the first 2 years of life, especially in critical areas of speech, language, and social interaction (Egeland & Farber, 1984; Egeland & Sroufe, 1981). The importance of the early parent-child relationship is thus underscored by these findings, especially because they may represent the possible beginnings of parent-child conflict, parental nonresponsiveness to infant demands, parental failure to provide stimulation and comfort, and infant characteristics that interact with parental ability.

Without consistent stimulation, comfort, and routine to aid in the formation of secure attachment, maltreated infants and toddlers have considerable difficulty establishing a reciprocal, consistent pattern of interaction with their caregivers. Instead, they show a pattern described as *insecure-disorganized attachment,* characterized by a mixture of approach and avoidance, helplessness, apprehension, and a general disorientation (Carlson, Cicchetti, Barnett, & Braunwald, 1989; Schneider-Rosen, Braunwald, Carlson, & Cicchetti, 1985). This insecure-disorganized pattern occurs much more often among maltreated samples of mothers and infants—as high as 80% (Carlson et al., 1989)—which is especially striking given that this pattern is very uncommon among nonmaltreated, middle-class samples (Main & Solomon, 1990).

Children's beliefs about themselves and others follow from their initial attachment experiences, so an insecure-disorganized pattern can have significant repercussions in later stages of development (Aber, Allen, Carlson, & Cicchetti, 1989). Importantly, children form complex mental representations of people, relationships, and the world during this period that influence their future thinking and behavior. Normally, their emerging view of themselves and their surroundings is fostered by healthy parental guidance and control that invokes concern for the welfare of others. Because such opportunities are seldom available to maltreated children, however, emotional and behavioral problems are more likely to appear as a result of their maladaptive view of themselves and others. Development of language and symbolic play also allows them to represent their growing awareness of self and other (Cicchetti, 1990), influenced by both maturational and environmental factors. Coster and Cicchetti (1993), for example, found that maltreated toddlers develop a communicative style in which language is used to complete various tasks (instrumental) but is used less frequently to accomplish social and affective exchanges. Maltreated toddlers showed a shorter mean length of utterance, suggesting that they engage in shorter periods of continuous discourse, demonstrate limited expressive (but not receptive) vocabulary during play sessions with their mothers, and display less communication aimed at exchanging personal information about themselves, such as talking about their own activities, thoughts, or feelings.

Some maltreated infants and toddlers become *hypervigilant,* looking for any cue related to a possible verbal or physical outburst (Crittenden & DiLalla, 1988), a further example of the impact of their unpredictable and at times fearful circumstances involving caregivers. Hypervigilance not only includes constant scanning of the environment but also developing the ability to detect subtle variations in adult behavior, such as facial, intonational, and body language, that alert them to possible danger (Herman, 1992). Sometimes they learn to placate angry parents to avoid becoming the target (Hennessy, Rabideau, Cicchetti, & Cummings, 1994). As disorganized toddlers become preschoolers, however, hypervigilance and similar ways of adapting to their environment give way to various forms of controlling behavior toward the parent(s). Controlling behavior may take the form of pseudomaturity, such as looking after the parent and the household, or emotional immaturity, such as excessive tantrums and noncompliance. This developmental transition among maltreated children—which differs significantly from nonmaltreated children—is believed to compensate for the absence of an expectable environment by controlling and organizing the parent (Main & Hesse, 1990). This explanation helps us to understand why maltreated youngsters are often described as more noncompliant at 24 months of age and more hyperactive, distractible, lacking in self-control, and emotionally volatile at 42 months (Erickson, Egeland, & Pianta, 1989).

Dysregulation of Emotions

Parent-child attachment and the home climate also play a critical role in emotion regulation, another early developmental milestone. Emotion regulation refers to the ability to modulate or control the intensity and expression of feelings and impulses, especially intense ones, in an adaptive manner (Cicchetti, Ganiban, & Barnett, 1990). Emotions serve as important internal monitoring and guidance systems designed to appraise events as beneficial or dangerous and to provide motivation for action. Emotions serve interpersonal regulatory functions as well, and emotional reactions and perceptions help young children understand their world (Bretherton, Fritz, Zahn-Waxler, & Ridgeway, 1986).

Most children learn emotional regulation naturally, through emotional expressions and explanations given by their caregivers. Abused children, in contrast, live in a world of emotional turmoil and extremes, making it very difficult for them to understand, label, and regulate their internal states. Expressions of affect, such as crying or signals of distress, may trigger disapproval, avoidance, or abuse, so maltreated youngsters have a greater tendency to inhibit their emotional expression and regulation (Cicchetti & Beeghly, 1987). When a new situation involving a stranger or peer triggers emotional reactions, they do not have the benefit of a caring smile or words from a familiar adult to assure them that things are all right. Anger modulation problems in the context of relationship conflicts have been found among samples of toddlers (Beeghly & Cicchetti, 1994) as well as among school-age children with maltreatment backgrounds (Shields, Cicchetti, & Ryan, 1994). Thus, emotional and behavioral problems shown by abused children can be explained on the basis of their attempts to regulate strong emotions, such as adopting a stance of compulsive compliance or remaining negative and resistant (Crittenden & Ainsworth, 1989).

An observed behavioral pattern among some younger physically abused children, labeled *compulsive compliance,* serves to underscore how early experiences can result in emotional overreactivity and unusual behaviors toward the caregiver (Crittenden & DiLalla, 1988). Compulsive compliance refers to a child's ready and quick compliance with significant adults, which occurs in the context of the child's general state of vigilance or watchfulness for adult cues. A child's compulsively compliant behavior may be accompanied by masked facial expressions, ambiguous affect, nonverbal-verbal incongruence, and rote verbal responses. Such behavior seems to emerge in pace with the child's abstraction abilities, at about 12 months of age, concurring with the child's ability to form a stable mental representation of the caregiver. Abused infants, it is believed, learn to inhibit behaviors that have been associated with maternal anger (e.g., requests for attention, protests against intrusions) and that, in toddlerhood, such children may actively behave in a manner designed to please their mothers.

Crittenden and DiLalla (1988) found compulsive compliance to predominate in physically abused and abused/neglected children, in response to a controlling, hostile, and punitive parenting style. Such increases in compulsive compliance, as well as cooperative behavior, are most evident from ages 1 year through $2\frac{1}{2}$ years among maltreated children, which contrasts with adequate-care children who usually display the normative independence-striving ("testing limits") behaviors expected of toddlers. Paradoxically, compulsive compliance may be adaptive in terms of reducing the risk of violence and increasing positive mother-child interactions during early childhood; however, this style may impair the child's long-term development due to the denial of strongly felt emotions and the relegation of self-experience and self-direction to a lower priority. This early pattern may lead to inflexible strategies of behavior, with the consequence of reduced reciprocity in interactions (Crittenden, 1992).

A recent study adds to an understanding of this unusual pattern of processing emotionally laden information at the level of brain activity associated with attention. Three pictures—happy, neutral, and angry adult faces—were presented at the same time to a sample of school-age maltreated and nonmaltreated children, who were randomly told to attend to each one to measure how they process affective versus neutral information. Compared with nonmaltreated controls, children with maltreatment histories showed more reactivity when asked to attend to the angry faces (Pollak, Cicchetti, Klorman, & Brumaghim, 1997). Reactivity was measured by event-related potentials in the brain, an index of central nervous system functioning thought to reflect the underlying neurological processing of discrete stimuli. The situational context—being asked specifically to look at the angry face—was found to be an important aspect of how such children attend to affective stimuli. This tendency to react more strongly to provocative stimuli may be adaptive in the short run, but it may create costly and maladaptive solutions that contribute to social-cognitive problems and adjustment difficulties of abused children over time (Pollak et al., 1997).

Perhaps one of the most far-reaching effects of maltreatment is the loss or disruption of the child's ability to regulate the intensity of his or her emotional feelings and impulses (Van der Kolk & Fisler, 1994). As they grow older and are faced with new situations involving peers and other adults, poor emotional regulation becomes more and more problematic. Modulation difficulties may also account for depressive reactions and intense angry outbursts shown among some abused children and adolescents, as discussed in later sections.

Deficits in Social Awareness and Peer Acceptance

In addition to emotion regulation, child abuse contributes to difficulty inferring emotional responses and behavioral intentions of others, which in turn can lead to maladaptive interactions with peers and dating partners (Rogosch, Cicchetti, & Aber, 1995), lower self-efficacy (Rogosch & Cicchetti, 1994), and peer rejection (Dodge, Pettit, & Bates, 1994; Salzinger, Feldman, Hammer, & Rosario, 1993). These relationship deficits carry over into adolescence, where those with a history of maltreatment have a limited ability to demonstrate basic relationship skills, such as empathy and positive, nonthreatening communication (Birns, Cascardi, & Meyer, 1990).

Empathy and Social Sensitivity. The development of empathy and social sensitivity to others during the preschool years are prerequisites to the development of positive, reciprocal peer relationships. Physically abused children, however, show little skill at recognizing distress in others, most likely because this has not been their experience. Early studies indicated that abused children performed more poorly than nonabused controls on measures of affective and cognitive role taking, social sensitivity, and the ability to discriminate emotions in others (Barahal, Waterman, & Martin, 1981; Frodi & Smetana, 1984; Straker & Jacobson, 1981). Laboratory studies similarly found that abused children have greater difficulty, relative to nonabused children, in identifying facial expressions depicting various emotions (During & McMahon, 1991). Together, these comparative studies pointed to deficits in social sensitivity and awareness that seem particular to children with maltreatment experiences.

Studies of peer interactions involving abused and nonabused children in naturalistic settings further established the importance of these underlying social deficits. A significant study by Main and George (1985) revealed how abused toddlers (although hypervigilant in regard to the feelings of adult caregivers) never exhibited a concerned response at witnessing the distress (e.g., crying, fearful) of another toddler, whereas the nonabused children responded with a concerned expression to one third of the distress events. Abused toddlers not only failed to show concern, they also actively responded

emerge in childhood, adolescence, or early adulthood, are examined more closely in the following section.

Affect Disturbance

Child abuse disrupts and impairs many significant childhood memories and experiences, which may account for the elevated symptoms of depression, emotional distress, and suicidal ideation among children with histories of physical, emotional, and sexual abuse (Kaufman, 1991; Koverola, Pound, Heger, & Lytle, 1993; Toth, Manly, & Cicchetti, 1992). Emotional trauma resulting from chronic rejection, loss of affection, betrayal, and feelings of helplessness that may accompany chronic maltreatment by one's own family members sets in motion attempts to regulate emotions and behavior, some of which may become adaptive and others that may not.

One of the more pronounced outcomes of child abuse is shown by elevated symptoms of depression, hopelessness, and lower self-esteem relative to nonmaltreated children and adolescents from similar socioeconomic backgrounds (Allen & Tarnowski, 1989; Downey & Walker, 1992; Kaufman, 1991; Kinard, 1995; Toth et al., 1992). Toth et al. (1992), for example, compared physically abused ($N = 46$), neglected ($N = 35$), and nonmaltreated children ($N = 72$), using several measures of depression and social adjustment (e.g., the Children's Depression Inventory [CDI]; Child Behavior Checklist). After controlling for age and cognitive functioning, the presence of depressive symptomatology was the only dimension that differentiated children from physically abusive homes and children from neglectful homes. More specifically, 22% of the children in the physically abusive group fit the clinical criteria for depression, compared with 6% of the nonmaltreated group and 3% of the neglected group. Drawing on attachment theory, Toth et al. (1992) suggest that children from abusive homes suffer reduced self-esteem due to harsh physical and verbal child-rearing methods that, in time, may develop into a more pervasive mood disorder. The findings serve to emphasize the damaging effects of maltreatment, specifically physical abuse, on the child's growing sense of self and the contribution that this dysfunctional development of self makes in the emergence of depression.

Kazdin, Moser, Colbus, and Bell (1985) also found significantly higher levels of self-reported depression and hopelessness and lower self-esteem among abused than nonabused child psychiatric inpatients, while controlling for major sociodemographic variables as well as the child's overall level of distress or severity of psychopathology. Furthermore, children with both past and current abuse were the most severely depressed, suggesting to the investigators that "a history of abuse retains its impact on the child and augments the effect of current abuse" (p. 305). The lack of affection, emotional rejection, and social isolation shown by abusive parents was believed to contribute to the child's risk of affect disorder. As with other clinical populations, perceived social support from mothers and peers may be an important factor for improving global self-worth and decreasing the likelihood of depression (Kinard, 1995). If symptoms of depression and mood disturbance go unattended, however, they are likely to increase during late adolescence and adulthood, especially among those who were sexually or physically abused since early childhood (Browne & Finkelhor, 1986; Kolko, 1992).

Related to the findings of affect disturbance is the possibility of posttraumatic stress disorder (PTSD), because physical abuse may qualify as a traumatic event for many children, unleashing strong emotional reactions and cognitive interpretations that last for years. Few studies have investigated PTSD symptoms among physically abused children, however, and the findings are equivocal (e.g., Pelcovitz et al., 1994). The common behavioral and social difficulties shown by abused children may mask some of the PTSD-related symptoms; alternatively, the traumatic impact may not emerge until considerably later in the life span, an interpretation supported by a recent follow-up study of adults who were physically abused as children. One third of adults who had been physically abused (based on a prospective sample of almost 1,200 maltreated children in total) met criteria for lifetime and/or current PTSD, a rate almost double that of a matched comparison sample of adults (Widom, 1998). PTSD symptoms, including vivid memories of traumatic events, attempts to avoid reminders of the trauma, and persistent symptoms of arousal among adults who were abused as children underscore the intensity and impact of early childhood abuse.

Violent and Antisocial Behavior

The intriguing but complicated connection between early maltreatment and the emergence of violent and antisocial behavior has been an important issue to the field. Child abuse has been significantly linked to arrest as a juvenile or adult (Widom, 1989b) or engaging in sexual and physical violence as a young adult, especially for males (Feldman, 1997; Malamuth, Sockloskie, Koss, & Tanaka, 1991). Correlational studies of the association between abuse during childhood and violent and antisocial behavior during adolescence note that the amount of violence in the adolescent's past best discriminates violent from nonviolent delinquents (Lewis, Pincus, & Glaser,

1979; Loeber, Weissman, & Reid, 1983; Tarter, Hegedus, Winsten, & Alterman, 1984). For example, Tarter et al. (1984) dichotomized the crimes of delinquents referred by juvenile court as assaultive or nonassaultive and found that 44% of the abused delinquents ($N = 27$) committed violent crimes, compared with 16% ($N = 74$) of the nonabused delinquents. Related findings were reported in a 40-year study of 232 males from violent and nonviolent low-income families (McCord, 1979, 1983), in which 22% of the abused ($N = 49$), 23% of the neglected ($N = 48$) and 50% of the rejected ($N = 34$) boys had been later convicted for serious juvenile crimes, such as theft, auto theft, burglary, or assault, compared with 11% ($N = 101$) of the boys from matched comparison families. A history of maltreatment is also associated with an earlier mean age at first offense, higher frequency of offenses, and higher proportion of chronic offenders (Widom, 1989a).

Widom's longitudinal study of a sample of 1,196 adults with known maltreatment backgrounds provides the strongest evidence of a connection between such experiences in childhood and current violent and antisocial behavior as adults. Consistent with the cycle-of-violence hypothesis, persons with histories of physical abuse (21%), neglect (20%), or both (16%) were particularly more likely to be arrested for a violent crime (Maxfield & Widom, 1996). Although not as visible as physical abuse, child neglect is linked to the cycle of violence, owing to the parent's disregard of basic child care and the violation of a child's dependency status, which may involve a parent's vehement refusal to provide for the child as well as a passive withholding of love and affection. This study also revealed that women with histories of physical abuse and neglect were significantly more likely than nonmaltreated women to be arrested for a violent act (7% vs. 4%, respectively), whereas this relationship was barely significant for abused and nonabused men (26% vs. 22%, respectively).

The connection between child maltreatment and subsequent violent or abusive acts has important implications. First, maltreatment poses major challenges to the child's cognitive, emotional, and behavioral coping strategies, yet many children and adolescents still remain capable of accomplishing major developmental milestones and become well-functioning adults. The pathway from child maltreatment to violent behavior—although very significant—is by no means direct, inevitable, or irreversible. Many circumstantial events, such as the availability of a caring adult, as well as individual factors, such as strong ego control, an easygoing temperament, and social competence, may play a role in mitigating such outcomes (Cicchetti & Lynch, 1995). Studies involving community as well as clinical samples of children attest to the reality that any form of child maltreatment can result in significant negative repercussions that persist into adulthood, including affect and behavioral disturbances, academic problems, and criminal and antisocial behavior (Mullen, Martin, Anderson, Romans, & Herbison, 1996). Although many—perhaps most—adults with histories of maltreatment lead productive and satisfying lives, the lives of others can be fraught with serious psychological distress and disturbance.

Beyond evidence of violent behavior, the consequences of child abuse have been described in terms of increased risk for antisocial personality disorder among men and increased risk of alcohol-related problems among women (Duncan, Saunders, Kilpatrick, Hanson, & Resnick, 1996; Luntz & Widom, 1994). Remarkably, even the amount of "routine violence"—frequently being hit with objects or physically punished—one experiences as a child is significantly associated with violent delinquent behavior later on (Straus & Donnelly, 1994). Although correlational, this finding has troubling implications given that corporal punishment is commonly used in North American society. The premise that growing up with power-based, authoritarian methods can be toxic to relationship and social patterns—even if such methods don't amount to physical injuries or identified maltreatment—remains tenable.

SUMMARY

This chapter has discussed the circuitous and unpredictable manner in which child maltreatment is believed to affect children's behavioral and emotional expression, as well as their cognitive view of the world. Child maltreatment can have a profound effect on normal development, disrupting the normal course of growth and adaptation. Like a row of dominoes, failure to develop an adaptive attachment strategy sets off a chain reaction that leads to unpredictable outcomes. The absence of an organized attachment strategy makes the young child's behavior more difficult to manage, which in turn causes the caregiver to react with even more withdrawal or abuse. A damaging, interactive pattern may develop that, over time, places the child's development in further jeopardy. Difficulties in early attachment and affect regulation, a distorted view of oneself and others, and peer problems and school adjustment are some of the major developmental consequences identified among this population. Chronic problems and clinical disorders are also more common among abused children and adolescents, particularly academic problems, behavioral and emotional disorders, and criminal and antisocial behavior. Fortunately, this process is neither inevitable nor irreversible. Many children who experience such events in infancy and early childhood manage to adapt successfully over the long run, reminding us that development is sensitive to positive as well as to negative influences.

NOTE

1. I am indebted to students and colleagues for their input into this conceptual model of theoretical pathways stemming from child maltreatment. Alphabetically, they are Carolyn Grasley, Anna-Lee Pittman, Deborah Reitzel-Jaffe, Katreena Scott, and Christine Wekerle.

4

UNRAVELING THE CAUSES I

Theory and Background

Child abuse was first recognized as a serious problem in the early 1960s, launching scientific efforts to understand the psychological makeup of parents who harm their own children. Because the vast majority of parents are capable of dealing with the demands of their role without resorting to power assertion or violence, concerns that abusive parents lack some form of inner control, show little concern about their role as parents, or have distorted beliefs about the importance of harsh discipline have received serious attention. Although many of these suspicions have been at least partially supported, a *distinctive* psychological profile of abusive parents—one that clearly accounts for differences between abusive and nonabusive parents—seems elusive.

Distinctive psychological characteristics of abusive parents may not exist because child abuse is a relational event that depends, to some extent, on situational factors that elicit parental reactions. Personality characteristics of abusive parents are broad ranging, just as they are for other groups of individuals, and by themselves cannot readily account for particular outcomes, such as physical violence. Studies of abusive parents, for example, find that they share many common psychological and situational features, but not many of these features differ significantly from sociodemographically matched groups of nonabusive parents (Wolfe, 1985). These findings suggest that attitudinal, behavioral, emotional, and cognitive variables may not significantly distinguish abusive parents from others, leaving us about where we started.

On the other hand, several important distinctions between abusive and nonabusive parents have been found that help to identify possible causal influences in greater detail. Many abusive and neglectful parents have little

probability of aggressive behavior. This process, therefore, bears some resemblance to other forms of problem behavior that develop over time as a result of ineffective or inappropriate responses to stressful or commonplace demands, such as drug and alcohol abuse.

The second presupposition required of this model relates to the importance of psychological processes linked to the expression of anger, arousal, and coping reactions in adults. These processes are responsible for determining the positive or negative outcome at each successive stage in the development of the parent-child relationship. They include operant and respondent learning principles for the acquisition and maintenance of behavior, cognitive-attributional processes that influence an individual's perception and reaction to stressful events, and emotional conditioning processes that determine the individual's degree of physiological arousal, perceived discomfort, and self-control under stressful circumstances.

These psychological processes, singly and combined, may accentuate or attenuate the impact of any of the major factors associated with child abuse. A parent who is reinforced (by the cessation of aversive child behavior) for using harsh physical punishment, for example, may continue to emit such behavior under similar circumstances, even in the absence of many of the additional high-risk factors. At the other extreme, a parent who is inundated with highly stressful demands, such as low-income housing, several difficult children in the home, or nonsupportive relatives, could escape from the pitfalls that lead to abusive behavior if he or she has learned very effective coping responses that serve to protect against the aversive impact of these events, such as positive child management skills, relaxation and distraction techniques, and problem-focused coping that serve to reduce arousal and perceived stress. Therefore, different outcomes to child abuse risk factors are clearly possible when the psychological resources of the individual and the family are taken into consideration, which is the premise for psychologically based interventions discussed in Chapter 6.

The course of the development of abusive behavior has been conceptualized by stages in the transitional model, shown in Figure 4.1. This figure provides an overview of the destabilizing and compensatory factors described below. The course initially begins with the parent's own preparation, in terms of psychological and social resources, modeling and similar learning experiences from childhood, and current style of coping with daily competing demands on one's role as a parent. Problems in these areas may then lead to poor management of acute crises and provocation that heighten parental anger, arousal, and level of discomfort. When this point is reached, which

Destabilizing Factors	Compensatory Factors

Stage 1:
Reduced Tolerance for Stress and Disinhibition of Aggression

- Poor child-rearing preparation
- Low sense of control and predictability
- Stressful life events

- Socioeconomic stability
- Supportive spouse
- Success at work and school
- Social supports and healthy models

Stage 2:
Poor Management of Acute Crises and Provocation

- Conditioned emotional arousal to child behavior
- Multiple sources of anger and aggression
- Belief that child's behavior is threatening or harmful to parent

- Improvement in child behavior
- Community programs for parents
- Coping resources

Stage 3:
Chronic Patterns of Anger and Abuse

- Child habituates to physical punishment
- Parent is reinforced for using strict control techniques
- Child increases problem behavior

- Parental dissatisfaction with physical punishment
- Child responds favorably to non-coercive methods
- Community restraints/services

Figure 4.1. A Transitional Model of Physical Child Abuse

may occur early in the development of the parent-child relationship or after a long period of reasonable stability, the parent may become overwhelmed by the amount and intensity of uncontrollable events. The child's behavior or characteristics serve as the triggering event that unleashes a floodgate of anger and frustration that leads to abuse; persons or things other than the child may likewise trigger an episode of anger and aggression, such as a co-worker, spouse, neighbor, household pet, and so on. Finally, a habitual pattern of irritability, arousal, and/or avoidance of responsibility may become established, which serves to perpetuate the use of power assertive or uninvolved child-rearing methods.

Reduced Tolerance for Stress and
Disinhibition of Aggression (Stage 1)

What factors initially play a role in setting into motion a malignant cycle of parent-child relations? Because it is unlikely that child abuse suddenly erupts from a placid family environment, we need to look at the processes suspected to remove the parent's inhibition to use excessive force against a child.

First of all, it is important to consider the manner in which such inhibition of aggression is initially established. If one assumes that the capability of using aggressive or coercive behavior is innate, its individual expression is most likely regulated to a certain extent by environmental forces (Bandura, 1973). Accordingly, appropriate inhibition typically evolves throughout childhood and early adulthood as the individual learns to discriminate between aggressive and assertive behavior, to develop self-control abilities, and to use prosocial means of attaining his or her goals. Because these counter-aggressive abilities are learned in large part through family interactions, it stands to reason that the family of origin is a prime suspect in the initial failure to establish inhibitory controls for aggressive behavior. This assumption is supported by studies showing the abuser's family of origin as a training ground for interpersonal violence and lowered social competence (described in Chapter 5). This training is inadvertently accomplished through the well-known principles of learning and social cognition. These principles involve modeling of aggressive problem-solving tactics via marital violence and corporal punishment, rehearsal and reinforcement (or lack of effective punishment) of aggressive behavior with siblings and peers, the absence of opportunities to learn appropriate problem resolution approaches, and the establishment of a cognitive viewpoint that adheres to strict family roles and low self-efficacy. All of these processes have been linked to the disinhibition, or increased expression, of aggressive behavior in other populations (Bandura, 1973; Patterson, 1982; Zillman, 1979) and are relevant to child abuse as well (Vasta, 1982).

These learning experiences in childhood and early adulthood increase the likelihood of creating a *predisposition* toward aggressive behavior under circumstances that resemble the original conditions in some fashion (e.g., similar affective arousal or behavioral goals were witnessed or directly experienced at an earlier period). But what factors now play a critical role in mediating the expression of aggressive behavior once the individual becomes a parent? The transitional model maintains that the response to noxious events can be markedly altered by psychological factors. This is essentially stating that the parent's response to the child is a function of the interaction between level of external stress and level of internal tolerance/coping. If stress is low and/or tolerance is high, such as when the child is playing quietly in a manner that pleases the parent and the parent has had an easy day, the parent's response may be quite acceptable. When reversed, such as the child demands to watch television and the parent is very tired and wants to be left alone, inhibition of anger and aggression may be weakened.

Levine (1983) identifies three psychological factors that have been most consistently linked to adult responses to stressful events: (a) control, or the ability to make coping responses during stress; (b) the amount of feedback or information one receives following an aversive event or the response to that event; and (c) the degree of predictability one has of the stressor. Control is often considered to be the most important psychological factor mediating the impact of stress (Lefcourt, 1973), for it allows the individual to avoid or escape the undesired event. As Levine (1983) sums up this relationship, "Having control is helpful, losing control is aversive, and previous experience with control can significantly alter the ability to cope with subsequent aversive stimuli" (p. 115). Feedback also serves a facilitative function in managing stress, because it conveys to the individual whether he or she has done the right thing and whether or not it has been effective. Predictability, on the other hand, is less clear-cut but seems to be related to the individual's *sense* of control; that is, an event may be perceived as less stressful if one believes that he or she can exercise personal choice, which is predicted on the basis of prior experience.

What implications does this knowledge have for an understanding of child abuse in its early stages? First of all, it is important to restate the significance of the parent's ability to cope with fluctuating levels of stress. Successful coping sets the stage for a more successful parent-child relationship, whereas coping failure early on sets in motion further debilitation of the relationship. We know from related research with other adult-clinical populations that stressful life events play a significant role in provoking the onset of suicide, depression, neurotic disorders, and health-related disorders (Brown & Harris, 1978). The common, everyday problems related to marriage, work, and personal accomplishment or rejection seem to have a greater influence on behavior in the long-term than the major crises, such as severe illness or financial ruin (Rutter, 1983). Thus, it is reasonable to assume that a similar process may be operative in the establishment of abusive patterns of inter-action: Stressful life events may provoke abusive or neglectful responses on the part of parents who are predisposed to such behavior through prior learning experiences. In addition, the three factors noted above can also influence the expression of aggressive behavior in persons who are predisposed to such behavior. In fact, the use of power-assertive or aggressive tactics with family members may be easily viewed as a successful, albeit inappropriate, method of attaining control, feedback, and predictability on the part of the user, thus establishing a persistent pattern of coercion.

Poor Management of Acute Crises and Provocation (Stage 2)

Stage 2 represents the hypothetical point in the development of abusive behavior in which the parent's previous attempts or methods of managing life stress and child behavior begin to fail significantly in their effectiveness. During the previous stage (which some parents may continue with indefinitely while others pass through rapidly), the parent has often acquired his or her own style of coping or dealing with the mounting stresses that accompany the role. Typically, these methods involve short-term and self-defeating solutions to one's problems, such as excessive alcohol or drug usage, frequent relocations (for employment, to escape debtors, etc.), harsh punishment of the children, palliative medications, and so forth. Once parents reach the point where they begin to recognize the futility or ineffectiveness of their efforts, a major issue becomes the real or imagined *threat* to their remaining control over the child, other family members, and related aspects of their life. Negative feedback and poor control and predictability of child-rearing and family matters all serve to exacerbate feelings of *losing control,* a term that many abusive parents use to describe their feelings leading up to an abusive episode.

At this juncture, the risk of child abuse rises sharply. In the face of mounting stress and pressure that has not been effectively resolved, the parent may at first conclude that he or she needs to step up the intensity of the punishment and power assertion that is showing signs of weakness and failure. This decision to increase punishment or aversive control can be described more precisely as a split-second response to perceived threat and provocation that has not been attenuated by other intrinsic or extrinsic feedback. In other words, the parent's behavior is momentarily irrational with respect to its intention, expression, and intensity.

Two psychological processes are particularly relevant to our understanding of this escalation from punishment to abuse: (a) the effects of mood states and emotional arousal (e.g., increased sensitivity to stimuli, agitation) and (b) the parent's perceptions of areas of stress related to child rearing (e.g., perceived loss of control, placement of blame for feelings of discomfort), both of which serve a radical function in the disinhibition of aggression. The following section describes the role of these processes in relation to the parent's response to the child's behavior.

The Effects on Aggression of Mood States and Arousal. A baffling question that arises in attempts to comprehend abusive behavior is how parents can overreact so strongly to their child's behavior or, conversely, why children receive the brunt of their parents' anger and rage. Social-psychological studies regarding the primacy of mood or affect on behavioral responses and studies on the development and expression of aggressive behavior offer some insight into this relationship.

It is not surprising to find that an individual's behavior can be greatly influenced by his or her mood. Laboratory studies of this relationship have shown that when a positive mood is artificially induced, people are better able to postpone gratification and are more willing to comply with the requests of others (Maccoby, 1983). Even more salient to the study of child abuse is the discovery that experiences can have affective "tags" when stored in memory. When these experiences are recalled at some later point in time, the recollection of the actual event is biased by the person's mood at that time. In a similar manner, if a person's current mood is one of sadness or depression, he or she is more likely to recall other previously sad or depressing events (Bower, 1981).

It may be deduced from this literature that the behavior of abusive parents is affected by the association between the child's current problem behavior and similar circumstances from previous stressful encounters. A parent's previous mood of distress and anger toward the child is recalled by the child's current behavior or expression, leading to an overgeneralized (i.e., more angry, more aggressive) response by the parent. In effect, the parent's affective state at the time of an aversive encounter with the child is *classically conditioned* to particular aspects of the child's behavior and/or appearance, such as voice tone, facial expression, or loud crying. When these child behaviors return, the conditioned emotional response of anger, irritation, or rage quickly reappears and contributes to the parent's inability to maintain self-control and rational thought. Presumably, the adult is responding to cues that have been previously associated with frustration or anger, and the adult's behavior toward the child may be powerfully influenced by these conditioning experiences (Berkowitz, 1983; Vasta, 1982).

Part of the answer to why a child may become the victim of unmitigated anger and aggression from the parent also comes from experiments with normal subjects. These studies have determined that anger, which is a precursor of aggression, is a highly interpersonal emotion that typically involves a close affectional relationship between the angry person and the target (Averill, 1983). The person's level of arousal and his or her beliefs about the *source* of arousal play a critical role in determining the actual expression of aggression. A person may become aroused, such as hyperalert, tense, anxious, or in a state of high emotion, from a number of sources, including frustration, extraneous physical arousal from exercise or exertion, or threat. If the person is provoked by someone or something following arousal from one of the above sources, aggressive behavior is more likely if the person is unaware of the source of the extraneous arousal and misattributes it to the current provocation, such as the child's behavior. This process has been termed *transfer of arousal* (Averill, 1983) and may account for episodes of abuse that occur in response to mild provocation from the child or spouse. An abusive parent may become angered and aroused by a previous encounter with someone else (an employer, neighbor, motorist, etc.), which lowers his or her threshold for anger and aggression with family members.

In brief, a person must believe he or she has a reason to be angry or must have some form of justification for anger. Averill (1983) maintains that a vicious cycle is formed between anger and aggression: Feelings of anger, often derived from various sources, create a need for justification. Once the anger has been justified, for example, by blaming the child for causing the parent to feel angry, upset, and hassled, this justification in return encourages further anger and aggression. As arousal turns into physical punishment or aggression, such behavior may be prolonged, and the act itself can become invigorating or cathartic. Arousal is reduced only if the attack is continued to the point of exhaustion (Zillman, 1979). Thus, negative arousal interferes with rational problem solving and reduces one's ability to control aggressive or excessive reactions (Vasta, 1982). However, because arousal itself is normal, cognitive-behavioral processes such as attribution for arousal and awareness of alternative, nonabusive responses are essential components in understanding why, under similar circumstances, some parents become abusive and others do not. Factors that influence the parent's level of anger and arousal, furthermore, may have a cumulative and multiplicative effect over time, thus underscoring their importance in preventing the recurrence of abuse.

Perceptions of Areas of Stress Related to Child Rearing. How a parent views child-rearing situations or evaluates and copes with life changes relates to how effective or adaptive that parent is in promoting child compliance and development (Kaplan, Eichler, & Winickoff, 1980). For this reason, the evaluative processes a parent goes through to conclude that the interaction with his or her child is stressful or nonstressful merit consideration. To address this concern, evaluations of parent-child interactions from the vantage point of appraisals of stress are considered, based on related clinical research.

The transactional model of stress (Folkman, 1984; Lazarus, 1981) describes a twofold process by which a person evaluates a situation as stressful. First, the person evaluates a specific transaction with respect to his or her own welfare (e.g., one's happiness, contentment, prosperity), and second, he or she evaluates coping resources and options. Stressful appraisals are those in which the outcome is viewed as involving some degree of harm, loss, threat, or challenge. Appraisals of harm, loss, or threat are characterized by negative emotions, whereas a challenge is characterized by pleasurable emotions, such as excitement and eagerness. Once again, a crucial factor that accounts for these distinct outcomes is the degree of control one believes he or she has over the situation; events that are seen as being out of the person's control are perceived as harmful or threatening, whereas others that are viewed as being within the person's control are challenging.

This stress model has apparent value in understanding the cognitive processes affecting the likelihood of child abuse. During Stage 2 of the development of abusive behavior, the parent begins to view familiar, difficult interactions with the child as being "out of control" and as a deliberate attempt to defy the parent's authority (Feshbach, 1980). Transgressions and annoyances perceived by the recipient as being deliberate evoke significantly more aggression than behaviors appraised as accidental (Shantz & Voyandoff, 1973). Even if the child is relatively compliant and well mannered, the abusive parent may view other aspects of the environment as highly demanding and, therefore, unjust. As a consequence, when the child cries or fusses to seek attention or assistance, the parent may appraise the situation in such a way that leads to a conclusion of provocation by the child (LaRose & Wolfe, 1987). Such an appraisal, in turn, can lead to justification for using excessive physical punishment to gain control over at least some aspect of his or her stressful and unsatisfactory situation.

Chronic Patterns of Anger and Abuse (Stage 3)

Even though some incidents of child abuse are relatively isolated, one-time episodes that have few of the historical and contemporaneous warning signs discussed herein, the more typical pattern of abuse involves a history of difficult parent-child relations, strained family relationships, and chronic levels of stress and inadequate resources. For this reason, the process that transforms stressful circumstances into abusive or high-risk practices, unfortunately, seldom reverses once the parent has failed in his or her attempt to manage the child or react to stress with physically coercive methods. Instead, a chronic, escalating pattern of anger and abusive behavior becomes established.

Stage 3 involves the repetition of provocative stimuli, such as child behavior problems, and the escalation of the parent's response to such stimuli in terms of intensity, frequency, and duration. Occasional stressful events, such as those mentioned in Stage 2, become more commonplace, and the adult's ability to adapt to the onslaught of constant disruption and negative events becomes more impaired. A habitual pattern of stress, arousal, and overgeneralized responses to the child and other significant persons becomes entrenched, often despite parents' self-perception that they are doing everything within their power to reverse this process.

Feelings of hopelessness and helplessness may surface, as a recognizable sign of the entrapment resulting from repeated failure and frustration (e.g., "No matter what I do, he won't listen!"). Alternatively, parents may express rigid adherence to their belief that everything will rapidly disintegrate if they loosen the grip that keeps them in tenuous control of the stress in their lives (e.g., "He only listens to me if I yell and threaten to let him have it!"). The parent-child relationship has had ample opportunity to be shaped through aversive control procedures, and both members find it difficult to escape from this style of interaction.

There is certainly some element of truth in parents' perceptions that they are trapped into continuing to use harsh forms of control with their child. Some children easily habituate to existing levels of punishment intensity so that more and more harsh forms of discipline are required to attain the previous level of compliance or desired behavior (Patterson & Cobb, 1973). Moreover, short-term consequences may serve to maintain a parent's strict control over his or her child. For example, strict control over the child may ease the parent's tension and frustration (through negative reinforcement) and provide him or her with immediate obedience from the child. These immediate gains may outweigh the less noticeable, long-term consequences of this negative cycle: (a) the need to increase the intensity of the punishment to maintain strict control, (b) the child's avoidance of the parent and susceptibility to emotional and physical harm, and (c) the failure of this process to teach the child the desired behaviors that would eliminate much of the need to rely on punishment methods.

Compensatory Factors

The accumulation of negative events and poor coping responses that lead, over time, to the increased probability of child abuse depend to some extent on the absence or failure of important compensatory factors. Clearly, many parents who face socioeconomic pressures and poor preparation for the parenting role are not entirely consumed by these processes. Although the potential number of compensatory factors is limitless, several highly significant ones can be identified on the basis of the parenting and child abuse literatures (Belsky, 1984; Maccoby & Martin, 1983; Wekerle & Wolfe, 1993).

During the early formation of the parent-child relationship and the initial establishment of a parenting style (Stage 1), financial and marital stability within the family unit certainly portends a more successful and favorable outcome. A supportive spouse may be capable of offsetting some of the confusion and irritation that the other parent may express in attempting to meet his or her role demands and own expectations. Adequate social supports, positive parenting models, and suitable resources also frequently accompany families who have stabilized their financial situation and have settled into the community. Along these same lines, parents who experience success and mastery in their educational and career goals are accomplishing tasks that have a bearing on their self-esteem, self-efficacy and, ultimately, on their sense of parenting competence. During Stage 1, therefore, these major factors can play a significant role in counterbalancing the stressful nature of family and child-rearing responsibilities.

Stage 2 represents a period in which stressful circumstances are having a significant impact on the parent's interactive style with the child. The degree of stress experienced by the parent, however, can be readily offset by factors in the family, the community, or those related to the parent's approach to coping. Improvement in the child's behavior represents one of the most highly salient compensatory factors during this period. For example, the child's behavior may improve, through maturation, treatment, change in family circumstances, or similar events, leading parents to reduce their use of strict control and to associate the child with pleasant events and attractive characteristics. The community may offer resources to the family that accelerate improvement in parent-child relations, such as subsidized day care facilities, educational and treatment programs for parents and children, employment training opportunities, and so forth. Notably, the parents' evaluation of their coping resources, options, and the potential for control of stressful events can have a significant compensatory effect. Folkman (1984) explains that coping resources may be psychological (such as problem-solving skills, an optimistic outlook, and high self-esteem), social (such as social support systems for emotional and informational needs), physical (such as stamina, energy, health), or material (such as money or transportation). Therefore, even if a situation is initially perceived as stressful, the overall impact of the event can be reduced if the appropriate coping resources are made available.

Compensatory factors are far and few between once a parent has progressed to the chronic abusive style denoted by Stage 3. Nevertheless, despite the propensity to justify the use of physical control techniques under a wide range of circumstances, such practices may be reversed by concerted individual, family, or community efforts (Melton & Barry, 1994). The parent, for example, may become dissatisfied with the outcome of physical punishment, either through the influence of others or through his or her own recognition, and feel an urgent need to refrain from using this method. Conversely, the child may mature and respond favorably to parental directives, and the coercive cycle may start to dissipate. Community efforts to curtail child abuse may also have an impact on the perpetuation of high-risk practices in some instances. This is especially evident when the parents are investigated for alleged abuse as soon as the crisis point has been reached and services are immediately put into place to supplement the parent's coping resources and reduce the level of stress. These compensatory factors augment one another so that the presence of several supportive resources stands the maximum chance of eliminating child abuse in any given situation.

SUMMARY

Unraveling the causes of child abuse requires an awareness of its unique context, including existing child-rearing norms that tolerate certain levels of violence between family members, adult risk factors, and triggering events that can turn an unpleasant encounter into an abusive one. This chapter reviewed three prominent theoretical viewpoints—psychiatric, psychological, and ecological—each of which adds important and unique contributions. A transitional model of abuse was described to account for the development and course of abusive child-rearing patterns. The model considers three transitional stages. The initial stage considers parents' own preparation in terms of psychological and social resources, what they learned from their own childhood experiences, and their style of coping with daily demands on their role as a parent. Parents who fail to deal with the realities of child rearing and become overwhelmed by the amount and intensity of uncontrollable events continue to the second stage, in which a child's behavior can trigger a floodgate of anger and abuse. If no resources or opportunities exist to compensate for this deteriorating pattern, a habitual pattern of irritability, arousal, and avoidance of responsibility may become established (Stage 3).

5

UNRAVELING THE CAUSES II

Multidimensional Influences

Current approaches to understanding child abuse emphasize the combination of individual, family, environmental, and social-cultural risk factors that can result in increased risk of maltreatment, as well as the possible protective mechanisms that disrupt this etiological process (National Research Council, 1993). Societal and cultural factors that influence the formation of a healthy parent-child relationship play a prominent role in child abuse, in addition to specific psychological processes affecting the dynamics of the relationship. The causes of child abuse, therefore, are best understood within the framework of a comprehensive systems model that accounts for how multiple layers of influence transform the ongoing parent-child relationship.

A multidimensional, systems approach to understanding child maltreatment is built on several underlying concerns (Wolfe & MacEachran, 1997):

- Abusive parents often lack the skills and resources necessary to cope effectively with child rearing and other stressful life demands, such as unemployment, crowded housing, and constant child attention. Ineffective parenting may, in turn, lead to a greater number of child behavior problems that progressively serve to increase parental stress and poor coping.
- In recognition of the range and intensity of identified problems among abused children, characteristics of the child that may be contributing to or maintaining the parent's abusive behavior are important elements to consider.
- Abusive behavior is a private and illegal act that occurs at a relatively low frequency, making it difficult to observe and study directly. Therefore, less extreme, routine interactions are often studied, such as parental commands, criticisms, and types of punishers; child demands, aversive behavior, and prosocial behavior. This approach to the study of such low-frequency

behavior assumes that everyday interactions and extreme violence are positioned at opposite ends of the same continuum (Friedman, Sandler, Hernandez, & Wolfe, 1981), as noted in Chapter 2.

• Although child abuse involves events between a parent and a single child, it is the case that such episodes are embedded within a network of family events. Therefore, it is necessary to study the entire family.

• An etiological model of child abuse and similar forms of maltreatment must include conceptually distinct levels of individual, family, and environmental factors. This involves investigation of critical antecedents, significant historical or developmental characteristics of the parent and child, the nature of the aggressive act and its impact on the child, the consequences that maintain such behavior, the nature of the family context, and the larger social system in which abuse occurs.

• This multidimensional paradigm is based on evidence that child abuse, like other forms of domestic violence, is seldom due to some extremely abnormal or pathological influence. To the contrary, child abuse is seen as the culmination of interrelated events both within and outside of the family. This argument provides the major basis for studying abusive behavior within a multilevel context of individual, family, and societal events. These events may be extreme forms of more everyday events and stressors that all families may experience to some degree.

The remainder of this chapter expands on theoretical explanations by considering findings regarding several key components in the etiology of child maltreatment, including individual, family, community, and social-cultural influences.

ADULT CHARACTERISTICS

A multidimensional approach to child abuse asserts that these phenomena are not explained on the basis of any particular event or single attribute of the parent or child. Rather, abuse is the product of multiple factors that potentiate one another in the absence of compensatory, protective factors or buffers (Cicchetti & Rizley, 1981). Child abuse involves a pattern of behavior rather than a psychiatric or personality disturbance. Behavior patterns specific to child rearing, such as managing difficult child behavior, problem solving with other family members, and handling chronic or acute episodes of stress define this population more accurately than categories of psychopathology (Wolfe,

1985). Individual characteristics of abusive parents are meaningful, however, if prior experience, current demands, and available alternatives are taken into account. A multidimensional, systems perspective of the interaction between contextual factors, child situations, and parental characteristics provides guidance for understanding the multiple causes of child abuse, and avoids overreliance on psychopathology as the principle explanation.

Adult characteristics associated with child abuse have been the subject of considerable research, organized herein in relation to the parent's childhood experiences, stress and coping abilities, distorted beliefs, child-rearing abilities and resources, and emotional reactivity. Major conclusions are presented for each of these areas.

Prior Maltreatment as a Child

Child abusers' experiences in their own families of origin were among the first issues to stand out in early clinical studies of such individuals (Kempe & Helfer, 1972). Because prior abuse and family violence in childhood may perpetuate a cycle of violence across generations, this issue remains an important, yet not fully resolved, concern. Also, the long-term effects of physical abuse and neglect on current child-rearing practices must be considered in relation to their associated psychological impact due to early parental rejection, lack of affection, exposure to dangerous situations, and similar negative experiences (Herrenkohl, Toedter, & Yanushefski, 1984). Physical abuse alone may not be the most significant factor in the backgrounds of children who repeat the cycle of violence, in that they usually have had many other experiences—some good and some bad—that affect this relationship.

With this caveat, the conclusion that abusive parents have themselves often been exposed to violence as children receives consistent support from retrospective studies of child abusers and violent delinquents reporting on their own backgrounds (Widom, 1989b). Abusive backgrounds significantly increase the likelihood that an individual will become subsequently involved in coercive relationships with peers (Dodge, Bates, & Pettit, 1990), dating partners (Malamuth, Sockloskie, Koss, & Tanaka, 1991; Wolfe, Wekerle, Reitzel-Jaffe, & Lefebvre, 1998), and their own children (Gaines, Sandgrund, Green, & Power, 1978; Straus, Gelles, & Steinmetz, 1980). Similarly, a multivariate examination of child abuse potential among a large sample of Navy recruit trainees (involving risk factors such as current partner violence, early childhood violence, and alcohol problems) found that childhood abuse experiences accounted for the most variance in explaining current child abuse potential among both females and males (Merrill, Hervig, & Milner, 1996).

Based on state records of offenses, coupled with detailed histories of child rearing, Straus and Kantor (1994) contend that maltreatment experiences (including milder forms of corporal punishment) are the single most significant risk factor for subsequent relationship violence in adulthood.

Based on similar studies, Kaufman and Zigler (1989) estimated that about 30% of child abuse victims carry the pattern into adolescence and adulthood. At the same time, they note that *most* child victims of maltreatment do not grow up to be perpetrators of violence, a finding often overlooked in terms of its potential to assist early prevention efforts to deter the cycle of violence. Abuse experiences in one's family of origin may create a *vulnerability* for further victimization by others, such as intimate partners, as well as a propensity to use power and control as a means of resolving conflict (Wolfe, Wekerle, & Scott, 1997). In addition to prior abuse experiences, the risk of becoming a victim or perpetrator of violence increases as a result of negative influences from peers (i.e., condoning violence), the absence of compensatory factors (such as success at school; a healthy relationship with siblings, friends, etc.), and the relative lack of alternative sources of information that serve to counteract existing biases, attitudes, and beliefs (Jessor, 1993). On the other hand, a number of positive influences, such as supportive adults within and outside the family, siblings, and successful school achievement, may serve over time to moderate the effect of abuse or other stressors in childhood (Rutter, 1979). Therefore, the significance of prior abuse, by itself, must be qualified by the recognition that the course is not inevitable, and many compensatory experiences can play a role in mediating this relationship.

Substance Abuse

Parental substance abuse has become recognized as an integral component of the multiproblem, abusive family. Although child abuse and neglect appear to have distinct sets of risk factors (Chaffin, Kelleher, & Hollenberg, 1996), substance abuse is common to both and plays a significant role in the onset as well as the continuation of maltreatment (Harrington, Dubowitz, Black, & Binder, 1995; Merrill et al., 1996). Compared with controls, parents of abused and neglected children are much more likely to report alcohol problems, from 18% to 45% across controlled studies (Widom, 1993). Substance abuse is also a significant outcome of the *effects* of early maltreatment in adulthood (Duncan, Saunders, Kilpatrick, Hanson, & Resnick, 1996) and has been linked to increased likelihood of re-reports (Wolock & Magura, 1996), which raises the possibility that substance abuse is an intermediary factor that increases the likelihood of perpetuating the cycle of violence.

Epidemiological studies support a substantial association between child physical abuse, neglect, and parental drug and alcohol abuse. A national interview study of 1,681 maltreating families revealed that almost 11% of respondents reported alcohol or drug dependence as a major family stress factor (American Association for Protecting Children, 1988). In a representative community sample of parents, lifetime alcohol or drug disorder occurred significantly more often among those who were considered to be abusive (40%) and neglectful (56%), compared with matched controls (16%) (Kelleher, Chaffin, Hollenberg, & Fischer, 1994). Notably, adults in this sample with an alcohol or drug disorder were 2.7 times more likely to endorse physically abusive behaviors and 4.2 times more likely to endorse neglect behaviors toward their children. The contribution of substance abuse disorders to predicting maltreatment remained significant after controlling for adult depressive and antisocial personality disorders, household size, and social support (Kelleher et al., 1994). Substance abuse, therefore, has been significantly associated with greater recidivism, danger to the child, permanent removal of the child by courts, and noncompliance with treatment (Wekerle & Wall, in press). The robustness and impact of this finding has led to calls for mandatory substance abuse screening in cases of serious child maltreatment as a necessary aspect of risk assessment and intervention (Murphy et al., 1991).

Cognitive Deficits and Distortions

Child abuse seldom involves isolated or premeditated events but, rather, occurs in the context of child rearing. Studies of the everyday interactions between abusive parents and their children, accompanied by knowledge of what abusive parents are thinking and feeling during these interactions, have afforded a useful understanding of the nature of these overt and covert processes. Descriptive, hypothesis-forming research efforts on the causes of child abuse, relying on observational studies of abusive and nonabusive families in the home and clinic, concluded that abusive parents express significantly less positive behavior during interactions with their children and other family members (reviewed in Wolfe, 1985; see Table 4.2). Relative to other families, members of child abusive families interact less often; when they do interact, the interaction tends to be more negative and to involve excessive forms of verbal and physical control that exceed the demands of the situation. Self-report measures further revealed abusive parents' unfamiliarity with their role as parents and expectations about normal child development and behavior (Azar, Robinson, Hekimian, & Twentyman, 1984).

The association between using aversive, power-assertive child-rearing strategies and cognitive deficits and distortions concerning children's behavior has led to concerted efforts to explain their connections. Cognitive deficits refer to an absence of thinking where it would be beneficial, whereas cognitive distortions refer to persons who typically do not lack the ability to organize or process information, but their thinking is described as biased, dysfunctional, or misguided (Kendall, 1993). Distorted or negative perceptions that relate specifically to the parent's own experience and/or perceptions of the child-rearing role may reflect the developmental immaturity first noticed among samples of abusive parents (Kempe & Helfer, 1972), which reflects the extent to which they accurately recognize the demands and responsibilities that accompany child rearing. Deficits and distortions may both play a role in parental perceptions and judgments of their child's behavior, perceptions that justify their coercive behavior. Abusive parents may misperceive or mislabel typical child behavior in ways that lead to inappropriate responses and increased aggression (Azar, 1997; Crittenden, 1993; Larrance & Twentyman, 1983; Milner, 1993). A parent may believe, for example, that there is "nothing wrong with punishing a nine-month-old for crying too much" (an item from the Parent Opinion Questionnaire; Azar et al., 1984), a cognitive deficit that can lead to harsh punishment.

Abusive parents not only perceive more child problem behavior and attribute responsibility and negative intent to the child, they also evaluate child behavior as being *very* wrong, to justify their severe disciplinary actions (Milner, 1993). Cognitive perceptions and distortion of events play a significant role in this evaluative process, based on previously learned expectations. The abusive parent interprets the child's behavior as being wrong and responds rapidly, without contemplating the circumstances or considering innocent explanations, which incites explosive, abusive reactions (Milner, 1993). Whether abusive parents *misperceive* child behavior, or whether they accurately perceive behavior but make different *evaluations and interpretations,* awaits further clarification.

A related social-cognitive explanation for this association between thoughts and actions centers on the power dynamics in abusive families. Parents who attribute high levels of power to children see themselves as victims of aversive child behavior (Bugental, 1993), which they perceive to be intentional and controllable by the child. This perception places the child in a tenuous position of control, which, in turn, leaves him or her vulnerable to parental efforts to counteract the child's power. Parental aversiveness and abuse derives from their threat-oriented schema of interpersonal relationships, which may have originated from their own relationship experiences (Sroufe & Fleeson, 1986). In response to perceived threat from their child, the parent may at first attempt to be superficially appropriate and ingratiating; however, if such an ingratiating style is unsuccessful, the parent switches rapidly to more power-assertive strategies, including physical action (Bugental, 1993). Given that aversive parental strategies do not sustain positive parent-child interactions, the groundwork is set for further escalation and coercive parent-child interactions, a conclusion supported by naturalistic (Bugental, Blue, & Lewis, 1990) and experimental studies of community samples (Bugental & Shennum, 1984).

Some parents apply the same faulty reasoning to themselves as well, which may explain why child abusers report lowered self-efficacy and more symptoms of depression (Chaffin et al., 1996). Sadly, these unrealistic expectations and negative-intent attributions can lead to greater punishment for child misbehavior and less reliance on explanation and positive teaching methods (Azar, 1991; Larrance & Twentyman, 1983). Children are seen as "deserving" of harsh punishment, and its use is rationalized as a way to maintain control. Thus, physically abusive parents may bring into interactions with their children a variety of negative beliefs and expectations about their children as well as about themselves as parents (Strassberg, 1995).

Anger and Arousal

Other than the act of physical assault, anger and arousal are perhaps the most distinguishing characteristics of abusive acts. Not surprisingly, child abuse researchers have consistently described abusive parents as impulsive and exhibiting a low frustration tolerance (see Tables 4.1 and 4.2). As mentioned in relation to the transitional model of abuse in Chapter 4, acts of interpersonal aggression are highly attributable to situational cues and characteristics of the individual (Averill, 1983; Berkowitz, 1983; Zillman, 1979). In the case of child abuse, the situational cues often involve aversive behavior or child features, and individual characteristics include factors such as oversensitivity (Knutson, 1978), disinhibition of aggression (Zillman, 1979), and limited interpersonal skills (Burgess, 1985). Physiological arousal (i.e., increased respiration, pulse rate, muscular tension) can lead to aggression, especially if the person labels the source of such arousal as anger provoking (Berkowitz, 1983). Moreover, negative arousal interferes with rational problem solving, such that the person's awareness of the intensity of his or her actions becomes blurred by the urgency of retaliation. This paired association between arousal and child behavior may occur gradually during everyday parent-child contact or struggles, or more suddenly, during highly stressful, difficult encounters.

Extending the procedures of laboratory studies of aggressive behavior, child abuse investigators measured abusive parents' emotional reactivity to difficult child behavior. Frodi and Lamb (1980) showed videotaped scenes of smiling and crying infants to abusive subjects and matched controls, anticipating that abusers would show greater discomfort, irritation, and emotional arousal in the presence of such stimuli. In response to infant cries and smiles, abusive subjects evidenced greater physiological arousal (i.e., increased skin conductance, blood pressure, and heart rate) and reported more negative affect (i.e., more annoyance and indifference and less sympathy) to both the crying and smiling infant scenes. Similarly, Wolfe, Fairbank, Kelly, and Bradlyn (1983) presented abusive and nonabusive parents with scenes of videotaped parent-child interactions, some of which were highly stressful (e.g., a child screaming and refusing to comply with her parent) and some nonstressful (e.g., watching television quietly). As hypothesized, abusive subjects responded to the stressful scenes with greater negative psychophysiological arousal than did the nonabusive comparison group (no group differences were found during the nonstressful scenes). These studies with child abusers, supported by numerous experimental studies of anger and aggression (see Averill, 1983; Berkowitz, 1983), support the contention that emotional arousal and reactivity play a crucial role in the occurrence of child abuse.

Emotional arousal by itself, however, is a normal and adaptive reaction to many situations, so the development of an abnormal pattern requires an awareness of other adult and situational characteristics that form a multidimensional explanation. Deviant arousal patterns most likely emerge as a function of an individual's predisposition, such as overreactivity and sensitivity to emotional cues, and prior learning experiences, such as exposure to violence as a child and other experiences of emotional distress noted in Chapters 3 and 4. Parental arousal can also be triggered by past memories associated with parents' own abuse or with previous conflicts with their child, events that may be highly specific to a particular parent-child relationship (Bower, 1981). Such memories and associations lead, of course, to an overgeneralized—more angry, more aggressive—parental response, because the parent is responding to cues that have been previously associated with frustration and anger.

CHILD AND FAMILY INFLUENCES

Family dynamics are important for explaining the range of psychological sequelae of abuse, because it often occurs in the context of multiproblem homes where poverty, parental psychopathology, alcoholism, and family dysfunction are influential (National Research Council, 1993). In a review of accidental and nonaccidental child injuries, poverty, family chaos and unpredictability, household crowding, and frequent residence changes were identified as characteristic of both unintentional child injury and child abuse and neglect cases, suggesting that there may be an amplification of the risk of multiple forms of maltreatment as the number of such stressors increase (Peterson & Brown, 1994). The frequent occurrence of stressful family circumstances and events, however, makes conclusions concerning *abuse-specific* causes and effects difficult to identify.

A pattern of compromise and undervaluing of children within the family can be seen across all forms of child maltreatment, whereby a common factor is the family climate of power assertion and authoritarian control. A climate of domination even extends to the social isolation of the family, and the social life of the child can be restricted as a result of the need to keep the home situation out of public view. Thus, the family context is generally described as one of insensitive, marginal parenting and harsh interactions (Friedrich, 1990), even though abusive parents and their children may sometimes behave appropriately under limited or superficial conditions (Crittenden, 1988).

Child Behavior

Questions concerning the child's role in increasing the risk of child abuse have received careful scrutiny, because abusive parents often attribute their anger to their child's behavior (Herrenkohl, Herrenkohl, & Egolf, 1983). Although children's behavior, physical features, or developmental limitations may increase the potential for abuse, no child characteristic—age, gender, temperament, low birth weight, hyperactivity, conduct problems, or handicapping conditions—has been associated with the risk of maltreatment *once environmental and adult factors are controlled* (National Research Council, 1993; Whitmore, Kramer, & Knutson, 1993). Importantly, children are not responsible for their own abuse in any manner; child abuse is an adult action that is never justified. Unintentionally, however, the child's behavior may still play a role in the continuation or escalation of an abusive or neglectful relationship.

Given the saliency of children's behavior to parental anger and aggression, it is not surprising that child behavior has been implicated as a major triggering factor to abusive episodes. Abusive incidents occur most often during difficult, but not uncommon, episodes of child behavior. A study of 825 official case records of physical abuse incidents revealed that abuse was most often associated with oppositional child behaviors, such as refusal, fighting and arguing, accidental occurrences, immoral behavior, dangerous behavior, the child's sexual behavior, and inconveniences because of the child (Herrenkohl et al., 1983). Interestingly, this study also revealed that circumstances preceding incidences of *neglect* were characterized more by chronic adult inadequacy as opposed to child behavior, such as refusing to meet family needs, inadequate adult supervision, parent's lack of knowledge, inappropriate use of medical facilities, unsafe home environment, and child's dangerous behavior. Not surprisingly, aversive child behavior, such as crying, may produce anger and tension in some adults that contribute to aggressive responding, as previously noted (Frodi & Lamb, 1980; Wolfe et al., 1983). These findings on the circumstances of abuse and the child's role are consistent with a multidimensional perspective that stresses the importance of both immediate and more distal contextual events.

Although research has attempted to unravel the influence of particular childhood physical and psychological impairments that may increase the risk to the child of being abused, the findings generally do not support a significant causal role (Ammerman & Patz, 1996). As noted, physically abused children have difficulty performing well at academic tasks, yet there is no clear evidence that they are more likely than nonabused children to have a specific learning disability or, vice versa, that children with learning disabilities are more likely to be abused (Caplan & Dinardo, 1986). Also, because physically abused children resemble some of the behavior patterns of children diagnosed with attention-deficit hyperactivity disorder (ADHD), investigators have considered a link between the two. One possible link would be the increased risk of harsh physical punishment toward children with ADHD, due to their more difficult and disruptive behavior. This connection was studied by Whitmore et al. (1993), based on the abuse histories and home environments of adult males who had been referred for ADHD-related problems and their nonreferred siblings. The findings indicated that the 14 ADHD children and their brothers did not differ in their reports of physical punishment, discipline, parental rejection, positive contact, or their general impression of their home environments. These findings, moreover, were generally replicated in a larger sample of 70 probands, 29 brothers, and 22 former classmates. The investigators conclude that ADHD does not evoke excessively punitive parenting, although they caution that the child's ADHD patterns may interact with certain parental characteristics to increase the risk of child abuse (Whitmore et al., 1993).

Marital Conflict and Violence

As mentioned in Chapter 1, interparental conflict and violence are often associated with child abuse. In their first nationwide study of violence, Straus et al. (1980) noted that marital disharmony and violence were significantly associated with higher rates of severe violence toward children (the researchers estimated that in approximately 40% of the families where the adults were violent toward one another, there was also violence toward a child at some point during a 12-month period). Comparative studies in the marital and child clinical literature further documented the relationship between adult conflict and increased child behavior problems (Cummings, 1997). This connection is logical, because the escalation of emotional arousal and aggression accompanying adult conflict (Jacobson et al., 1994) can easily carry over to interactions with the child. In fact, marital conflicts and violence most often arise during disagreements over child rearing, discipline, and each partner's responsibilities in child care (Edleson, Eisikovits, Guttmann, & Sela-Amit, 1991; Hilton, 1992). Children may be caught in the cross fire between adults, or in other cases, they may precipitate parental arguments and conflict by misbehaving (Jaffe, Wolfe, & Wilson, 1990). The child may be injured during attempts to interrupt parental fights or to escape from the situation, among other possibilities.

These circumstances can produce an escalating cycle of family turmoil and violence, whereby children's behavioral and emotional reactions to the violence create additional stress on the marital relationship and further aggravate an already volatile situation. Because of the physical and psychological consequences of violence, moreover, abused women are less capable of responding to their children's needs, which again increases pressure on the family system. Tragically, marital violence and family turmoil not only frighten and disturb children in a direct manner, but the resulting fallout from such events—ranging from changes in financial status and living quarters to loss of family unity and safety—prolongs the stress and harmful impact on children's development (Wolfe, Jaffe, Wilson, & Zak, 1985).

Social Isolation

One of the commonly noted features of abusive families is their social isolation, coupled with stressful living conditions, such as a lack of adequate day care, peer groups or close friends, and adequate housing (Garbarino, 1976; Thompson, 1994). Maltreating parents often lack significant social *connections* to others in the extended family, the neighborhood, the community, and to the social agencies most likely to provide needed assistance (Korbin, 1994). These factors play an indirect, yet significant, role in the early formation and healthy establishment of a positive versus abusive parent-child relationship. As a result, abuse and neglect are difficult to detect, and community agents who could promote healthy parent-child relationships are less likely to be influential. Added to this notion of social isolation is the concern that certain cultural factors, such as child-rearing practices, geographical distinctions, and kinship systems might serve as risk-enhancing or risk-reducing factors in child abuse and neglect.

Social isolation, however, is not a singular factor but, rather, a set of variables linked to the parent's perception of support and their informal and formal networks (Coohey, 1996). For example, an individual's perception of the degree of intimacy in his or her social network may serve as a barrier to stress (Henderson & Moran, 1983). Neglectful families are especially prone to such isolation and insularity, which may be tied to the parents' significant interpersonal problems (Polansky, Gaudin, & Kilpatrick, 1992). Moreover, rather than being a causal factor in the etiology of child maltreatment, social isolation may reflect the degree of an individual's or family's social competence in interpersonal and child-rearing situations (Burgess & Youngblade, 1988).

SOCIAL AND CULTURAL INFLUENCES

Intuitively, a primary focus on individual and family-level factors as causes of child abuse and neglect is very limiting; many contemporary societies face high rates of child maltreatment in relation to social conditions at the community and cultural level (Garbarino, 1997). In addition to proximal events directly linked to a particular abusive incident, an understanding of maltreatment must take into account many macrolevel factors suspected to be indirect precursors to abusive situations. The most prominent social and cultural dimensions contributing to maltreatment stem from poverty, social disadvantage, and the wide acceptance of corporal punishment.

Poverty and Social Disadvantage

Although child abuse is certainly not limited by the boundaries of socio-economic status, it must be considered in the context of poverty and environmental stress. Poverty is associated with severe restrictions in the child's expectable environment, such as lack of adequate day care, safety, and housing, which often impair or impede the development of healthy parent-child relationships. Collectively, structural determinants of a community's social organization, such as economic and family resources, residential instability, household structure, and neighborhood poverty, influence rates of child maltreatment more than any individual or family factor alone (Coulton, Korbin, Su, & Chow, 1995; Gil, 1970; Pelton, 1978). In an early study, for example, socioeconomic factors accounted for 36% of the variance in rates of child abuse in Pennsylvania (Garbarino, 1976). Unemployment (Light, 1973), restricted educational and occupational opportunities (Gil, 1970), unstable or violent family situations (Straus et al., 1980), and similar disadvantages (e.g., housing, privacy, noise and pollution levels) often associated with lower social class membership have all emerged as major sociocultural factors influencing rates of child abuse and other urban problems in North America (Coulton et al., 1995).

To explain this connection requires consideration of the psychological dimensions noted above. Social and cultural disadvantage amounts to an extra burden of stress and confusion and to few suitable alternatives. The coping abilities of family members are impaired by their circumstances and further constrained by their resources. One caution is in order, however. Despite these powerful socioeconomic forces, maltreatment appears to have a significant impact on child development above and beyond the influence of stressful socioeconomic circumstances alone (Kurtz, Gaudin, Wodarski, & Howing, 1993; Trickett, Aber, Carlson, & Cicchetti, 1991).

Corporal Punishment

Child-rearing practices have been changing dramatically over the past 50 years or so. Today's parents are expected to appreciate their child's developmental strengths and limitations and to move away from total reliance on disciplinary control methods toward ones that encourage the child's emerging independence and self-control (Maccoby & Martin, 1983). Differentiating child abuse from child discipline remains difficult, because cultural norms in many Western societies accept corporal punishment as a primary, even necessary, component of discipline. As a result of such wide acceptance, four of five 3-year-old children in the United States are physically punished by their parents in any given year, and about 1 in 10 receive such severe discipline that they are at considerable risk of harm (Straus & Gelles, 1990).

Many parents spank their children, even though they question its effectiveness (Gallup Organization, 1995). Most parents who use physical discipline are not abusing their children in either the physical or psychological sense. But a change in circumstances—increased stress, more difficult child behavior—can up the ante quite suddenly. Furthermore, acceptance of corporal punishment leaves it up to local standards and parental judgment to define what is reasonable punishment, because no universal standard exists.

Cultural values, historical precedent, and community standards, therefore, may set the stage for one person's abuse being another person's discipline (Korbin, 1994). Discipline also involves considerably more effort and planning than does punishment alone, and unfortunately, many parents are not familiar with, or have not learned to use, less coercive methods of discipline consistently. Thus, child maltreatment occurs to a certain extent because of limited cultural opportunities to learn about appropriate child rearing and to receive necessary education and supports, as well as because of long-held social customs that endorse the use of physical force to resolve child conflicts.

SUMMARY

Unraveling the causes of child abuse requires consideration of individual, family, community, and cultural influences and how they interact dynamically during the critical formation of the parent-child relationship. Abusive parents can be characterized as coming from multiproblem families of origin, where they were exposed to traumatic or negative childhood experiences such as family violence and instability. As adults, they are often incapable of managing the levels of stress found in their environment and tend to abuse alcohol and drugs, presumably in response to stressful events and poor coping ability. Lack of appropriate preparation for their role as caregivers, coupled with cognitive deficits and distortions about child rearing, may serve to make interactions with their child difficult and aversive. Repeated exposure to such aversive exchanges intensifies the parent's anticipation and emotional reaction to common child behaviors, affecting both their judgment and self-control. In addition to these important adult characteristics, child abuse must be considered in relation to its family and community context (parents' response to variations in child behavior, marital conflict and violence, social isolation). Social-cultural factors such as poverty and social disadvantage, child-rearing practices, and family privacy also influence the expression of child maltreatment.

6

PREVENTION AND TREATMENT STRATEGIES

Child abuse has been described in relation to harmful socialization practices that often have a pervasive impact on development. Ironically, most current approaches to intervention require that an abusive incident be discovered and reported before any efforts are put into place to assist; yet by that time, considerable harm may have occurred to a child's psychological development and well-being. Preventing child abuse early on is a more sensible option and is now a distinct possibility in view of acquired knowledge of the social and psychological risk factors. Based on the growing foundation of research findings and community initiatives, a top priority exists to formulate, implement, and evaluate the effectiveness of prevention-oriented programs for child abuse.

The increased understanding of the causes and impact of child abuse, coupled with advances in treatment methods for troubled families, provide optimism for planning prevention and early intervention programs. This chapter describes demonstration projects and ideas favoring the premise that a large proportion of abusive incidents and their associated outcomes can be prevented. Nonetheless, retooling from a detection and protection approach to a more prevention-oriented model of family assistance and support poses considerable challenges that require long-term strategies (Melton & Barry, 1994). As discussed in the closing comments below, there are no short-term or inexpensive solutions to child maltreatment, only gradual, meaningful steps that lead to progressive and lasting change.

THE SCOPE OF
CHILD ABUSE PREVENTION

Many of the developmental implications of child abuse relate to problems arising from perturbations in the parent-child relationship, a relationship that either was never well established from the beginning or that began to disintegrate during periods of developmental change or family stress. Therefore, an overriding goal of child abuse prevention from the perspective of healthy child development is to establish positive socialization practices responsive to situational and developmental changes. Healthy child-rearing practices serve to buffer the child against other socialization pressures that can be stressful or negative, and reduce parents' reliance on power-assertive methods that can become abusive (Maccoby & Martin, 1983).

The goal of improving socialization practices is well matched to the transitional model of child abuse presented in Chapter 4. Child abuse occurs most often during periods of stressful role transition for parents, such as the postnatal period of attachment, the early childhood period of increasing socialization pressures, times of family instability and disruption (e.g., divorce, single parenthood, change in caregivers), or following chronic detachment from social supports and services. Moreover, many of the risk factors leading to a gradual transition toward abusive socialization practices are more recognizable than in the past. Prevention and early intervention approaches make considerable sense for building resistance against many of the unavoidable pressures acting on high-risk families. The purpose of child abuse prevention, therefore, involves more than forestalling events that are harmful to a child; prevention can also involve actions that enhance something positive for children, especially an improved parent-child relationship (Wekerle & Wolfe, 1993).

Because child abuse is a learned behavior, elicited and maintained by a multitude of events that are coming into clearer focus, it can be prevented, presumably, by the availability of appropriate learning opportunities and resources. The goals of prevention involve the development of strong positive child-rearing abilities by strengthening the early formation of the parent-child relationship, improvement in the parent's abilities to cope with stress through exposure to a mental health support system, and the development of the child's adaptive behaviors that will contribute to his or her emotional and psychological adjustment. Approaches to prevention, early intervention, and treatment, therefore, should emphasize education and guidance in a format that is flexible and responsive to the needs of families and individuals. Moreover, intervention must be redirected toward the important issues that

families face during each of the emerging developmental stages that the child
and parent must endure, as opposed to attempting to repair the relationship
difficulties later on (Rosenberg & Reppucci, 1985).

Special Considerations

Intervention with maltreating families raises a number of special concerns
and considerations. The parents often approach psychological treatment in
much the same way as medical treatment, expecting the clinician to eliminate
the problem they are reporting (Azar & Wolfe, 1998). That they usually come
to the attention of professionals based on someone else's concern rather than
their own also merits consideration. They may be resistant to the goals of
therapy, unfamiliar with the course and nature of psychological treatments,
and confused by the explanations and information being provided on their
behalf. The result can often lead to less than a desirable outcome from the
perspective of both the client and the therapist.

Current laws and limited resources also dictate that treatment efforts are,
by necessity, delivered primarily to parents rather than children, regardless
of the child's developmental needs. Although parent-focused interventions
can also benefit children, there is a growing awareness of the need to provide
corollary services aimed specifically at the child's developmental deficits or
lags (see below). On the positive side, success and mastery on the parent's
part (in areas such as employment, social contacts, achieving more desirable
child behavior, etc.) are likely to have a powerful impact on child abuse
prevention and child development. Likewise, reductions in child-related
pressures and demands via subsidized day care and preschools, homemaker
programs, and stimulation programs facilitate the parent's mastery of events
that could otherwise become overwhelming (Barry, 1994; Fantuzzo, Weiss,
& Coolahan, 1998). Therefore, a major challenge of prevention becomes the
identification and selection of appropriate, desirable, and attainable goals that
can be addressed through community action programs, individual skills-
training efforts, and related therapeutic activities.

Drawing on major factors associated with child abuse that have been
discussed throughout this book, Table 6.1 summarizes the targets for child
abuse prevention and intervention in relation to individual, family, community, and cultural factors. The majority of these targets fall at the individual
child and parent level, such as poor coping skills, ineffective child-rearing
approaches, long-standing psychological problems, and others. However,
this emphasis on the individual should not be interpreted as a reflection of
the disproportionate weight that should be given to individuals as opposed to

TABLE 6.1 Multilevel Targets for Child Abuse Prevention and Intervention

---

Individual Level

  Child

    Deficits in social sensitivity and relationship development, which includes problems related to poor attachment formation, the development of empathy, and affective expression

    Cognitive and moral development, which refers to poor social judgment and school performance in particular

    Problems in self-control and aggression

    Safety and protection from harm

  Parent

    Symptoms of emotional distress, learning impairments, and/or personality problems that limit adult adjustment and coping

    Emotional arousal and reactivity to child provocation; poor control of anger and hostility

    Inadequate and inappropriate methods of teaching, discipline, and child stimulation

    Perceptions and expectations of children, reflected by rigid and limited beliefs about child rearing

    Negative lifestyle and habits related to the use of alcohol or drugs, prostitution, and subcultural peer groups, which interfere with the parent-child relationship

Family Level

  Marital discord and/or coercive family interactions and/or a history of violent male partners

  Chronic economic problems and associated socioeconomic stressors

  Social isolation and the inability to establish meaningful social supports

Community Level

  Adequate housing, safety, and schools

  Support and educational services for disadvantaged families

  Suitable employment opportunities

Societal and Cultural Level

  Alternatives to corporal punishment of children

  Parent education, preparation, and support opportunities

  Reduction in the unequal burden of child-rearing responsibilities placed on women

---

other aspects of the system. It could easily be argued, for example, that interventions that effectively reduce the adverse influence of socioeconomic conditions on families (such as subsidized housing and job-training programs) can have a significant impact on child abuse prevention as well (Eckenrode, Rowe, Laird, & Brathwaite, 1995).

Contributions From Prevention Science

From a health promotion perspective, prevention of child abuse can be achieved on the basis of primary, secondary, and tertiary efforts. Primary prevention of child abuse involves efforts to reduce the incidence of such events. These efforts are targeted at large segments of the population regardless of any signs or symptoms of concern. Identification of the most important groups to reach is guided by epidemiological studies that point to particular characteristics of the population who have the problem, such as persons living in disadvantaged neighborhoods (Melton & Barry, 1994). Primary prevention is population based rather than individually based, so its successful application is reflected by reductions in the rate of the disorder in the selected population, such as a particular community or county (Lorion, Myers, Bartels, & Dennis, 1994).

Secondary prevention of child abuse involves interventions that decrease prevalence by minimizing or reducing the severity and continuation of the early signs of abuse. In contrast to a population-based focus, secondary efforts are usually aimed at individuals who have been identified as showing clinical signs or characteristics likely to lead to problematic parent-child relations. Finally, tertiary prevention of child abuse involves attempts to minimize the course or prognosis of the problem. At this stage, the problem is already evident, and the goal of intervention is to restore the individual's optimum level of functioning. Such efforts include treatment services for adult offenders and child victims to prevent further episodes or occurrences. Tertiary prevention is the most familiar form of intervention for child abuse, because persons who already have the problem are easier to identify and, presumably, to assist. At the same time, however, tertiary efforts are expensive and less effective at reducing the incidence and consequences of psychological disorders (Albee, 1985). For child abuse and other issues affecting children and youth, secondary and primary prevention efforts are more attractive, because intervention at an earlier stage in the process may restore normal developmental pathways and minimize harm.

Prevention principles have been further clarified by *universal, selected,* and *indicated* strategies (Gordon, 1983; Institute of Medicine, 1989). Universal interventions are assumed to be generally positive and carry very low risk. Tailored to conform to subcultural norms and expectations, universal programs can contribute to healthy adaptation across various situations and developmental changes. Moreover, the proactive, positive nature of universal programs makes them more readily acceptable, avoiding the pitfalls sometimes associated with identifying certain persons or groups as being at risk

(Lorion et al., 1994). Selective interventions may be appropriate for members of particular subgroups who have been shown, through epidemiological studies, to have a heightened risk of developing psychological problems in adolescence and early adulthood. Given the saliency of the risk factors, specific interventions are justified on the basis that they can reduce potential harm. Third, indicated interventions can be offered to those who show, on an individual basis, clear indications that they are at risk for the undesired outcome. Such interventions are comparable to secondary prevention and tend to be highly focused, more expensive to deliver, and more intrusive than the other approaches. Again, however, their use is justified by evidence linking certain symptoms or behaviors (such as harsh child-rearing methods) to harmful outcomes (such as child abuse).

Although far from realized, child abuse prevention efforts have begun to organize around the principle of building on strengths and developing protective factors in an effort to deter violence and abuse. Some prominent examples of these efforts follow.

UNIVERSAL AND
SELECTED PREVENTION EFFORTS

Universal and selected prevention programs are often targeted at the broader community or societal level, in an effort to influence large numbers of people and the most significant causes and effects of child abuse. Rosenberg and Reppucci (1985) provide three examples of such strategies in reference to child abuse prevention: (a) competency enhancement, such as parent education programs; (b) public awareness and information services; and (c) interventions that target vulnerable populations during periods of transition and stress, such as parent aide and family support programs. These strategies are summarized in Table 6.2 in reference to their target populations, their timing, and the behaviors often targeted for preventative benefit.

Broad-scale efforts to enhance parental competency in large segments of the population offer a relatively inexpensive method for disseminating knowledge of child rearing. Such programs are usually delivered to large audiences or groups in an engaging and entertaining format, such as the use of live theater, television, or school classrooms. By soliciting the interest of the general public or identified cultural groups, programs with this philosophy can impart information on different parenting methods (e.g., the use of nonviolent punishment), child development (e.g., what to expect of small children), and coping strategies (e.g., seeking advice from others) that is

TABLE 6.2 Approaches to Universal and Selected Prevention of Child Abuse

Method	Target Population	Timing of Program	Target Behaviors	Examples of Content
Competency enhancement	General public; specific cultural groups; first-time parents and teens	Prior to or during transition to parenthood	Parenting skills, child development information; coping strategies	Use of live theatre and TV to impart parenting information to public
Public awareness campaigns; networking; crisis and referral services	General public; special census tracts of disadvantaged populations	Not necessarily linked to transitional periods	Understanding child abuse and how to seek help	Operation of community crisis lines; strengthening formal and informal helping networks
Family support programs for high-risk groups	Single and teen parents; low socioeconomic status or isolated families; parents of disabled children; parents undergoing crises	Pre- and postnatal periods; crisis periods	Parent-child attachment; prenatal health habits and visits to well-child clinics; positive child rearing; home safety	Parent aide is assigned to visit parents at risk to assist during transitional periods with advice, transportation

especially relevant for the transition to parenthood. Programs aimed at preventing the onset of abusive behavior, in comparison, focus more on increasing the general public's awareness and understanding of child maltreatment and ways to access important community resources. These methods include a variety of delivery formats, such as media campaigns, home-based services for families, and community networks that provide support and feedback to families.

Interventions that target vulnerable populations, such as single and teenage parents, low-socioeconomic status or isolated families, and parents undergoing crises, offer considerable assistance to these subgroups during pre- and postnatal periods and times of excessive stress. At the level of universal and selected prevention, such efforts are exemplified by local programs that assist identified high-risk families during transitional periods, such as hospital-based programs for improving early parent-child attachment, in-home parent aides who model effective parenting methods and provide child-rearing assistance, and trained health visitors who sensitize parents to the health and psychological needs of their children.

Model programs in this area have developed from the field of public health and nursing and involve universal efforts to provide education and support for new parents by home-visiting programs (Aronen & Kurkela, 1996). At the individual and family level, need for support, instruction, and resource links among new parents is best met by a personalized outreach strategy, such as home visitation. This approach is illustrated by the Prenatal/Early Infancy Project (PEIP) of David Olds and colleagues (Olds et al., 1997; Olds, Henderson, Chamberlin, & Tatelbaum, 1986; Olds, Henderson, & Kitzman, 1994), which began in the late 1970s. This team targeted first-time parents who possessed one or more child abuse risk factors, such as teenage parents, single parents, and low-income families. Child care services and pre- and postnatal nurse home visits were offered to establish resource links and child development education. Notably, individuals receiving this intervention are seen in terms of their strengths and abilities rather than their deficits, which translates into an empowerment strategy. Women are assisted in understanding and meeting their own needs and those of their newborn child and are taught skills necessary to enhance this relationship as well as their own self-development.

The encouraging findings from this prevention program support these methods of influencing major psychological determinants of healthy parent-child relationships. Relative to controls, mothers receiving the program developed or changed their understanding of child health and development, their expectations for their own development, and their self-efficacy. A

15-year follow-up with 324 mothers and 315 of their first-born adolescents revealed that this program of prenatal and early childhood home visitation by nurses can reduce subsequent pregnancies, use of welfare, child maltreatment, and criminal behavior among low-income mothers and children (Olds et al., 1997). Participants gained over controls on important dimensions of better family planning concerning number and spacing of children, less need for welfare (on average, 60 vs. 90 months of receiving government assistance), less child maltreatment (an average of .29 vs. .54 verified reports), and fewer arrests of their children during adolescence (an average of .16 vs. .90 arrests) (Olds et al., 1997).

Healthy Families America, an expansion and elaboration of Hawaii's Healthy Start Program, is another promising example of universal home visitation programs that emphasize child abuse prevention in the context of family assistance and support. This network of programs, currently being evaluated in 29 of its 270 sites across the United States, offers a comprehensive assessment of the strengths and needs of families at the time of birth, outreach to build trust relationships and acceptance of services, teaching problem-solving skills, expanding support systems and promoting healthy child development and positive parent-child relationships (Daro & Harding, in press). Current findings indicate that home-based intervention promotes a more nurturing environment in which mothers are more involved and sensitive to children's cues and use less punishment. In the Hawaii study, moreover, a lower level of child abuse risk and a lower incidence of child abuse and neglect was achieved (0% vs. 4.2%, treatment vs. control conditions, respectively) (Center on Child Abuse Prevention Research, 1996).

Universal and selected prevention efforts are clearly not a one-size-fits-all proposition. Such efforts offer several important advantages to dealing with child abuse, although these must be weighed in relation to the limited (but increasingly expanding) evidence of their effectiveness. Most significantly, these prevention formats are innovative, engaging, and more cost-effective as a means of imparting knowledge and increasing awareness of parental responsibilities (Britner & Reppucci, 1997; Leventhal, 1997). However, with the possible exception of the home visitor concept, the degree to which these approaches can actually prevent child abuse or enhance family functioning remains undetermined. Such approaches may be too far removed from the time of actual stress or may not be specific enough to assist those individuals who are in greatest need of assistance in parenting. Whereas such efforts to enhance positive experiences at an early stage in the development of the parent-child relationship hold considerable promise for the prevention of child maltreatment and its consequences, matching such efforts in a culturally sensitive and beneficial manner remains challenging (Daro & Harding, in press; Wolfe & Jaffe, in press).

INDICATED CHILD ABUSE INTERVENTIONS

Several intervention strategies have been developed to remediate major deficiencies in parenting skill, knowledge, or coping methods among the more seriously distressed subgroups of families. In contrast to universal and selected prevention, these approaches are most often targeted at the individual and family level of involvement and incorporate delivery formats (i.e., group and individual sessions) that best fit each family's needs and progress. Treatment components include parent- and family-centered approaches, such as child management training, parent education and support groups, anger and stress management, and methods for treating conditions in the family that precipitate abusive episodes (e.g., marital problems, substance abuse). Although less common, child-centered approaches are also emerging in conjunction with family- and community-based efforts.

Table 6.3 summarizes the aforementioned approaches to child abuse early intervention and treatment in reference to target populations, timing, and behaviors targeted for intervention. What stands out among the four parent- and family-centered approaches is their focus on particular skill or knowledge deficits among somewhat overlapping target populations. With the possible exception of parent education and support groups, these approaches are intended to modify existing or formative patterns that are highly problematic for the parent and child. For example, parents who require concrete demonstration of methods to promote child compliance, are socially isolated, or demonstrate anger control problems are offered individual or group intervention designed to teach skills such as nonviolent discipline methods, self-control, and ways to access community resources.

Parent- and Family-Centered Approaches

Treatment of child abuse and neglect can be delivered in a number of ways: to individual parents, children, parents and children together, or to the entire family (Becker et al., 1995). No matter how it is delivered, treatment of physical abuse usually attempts to change how parents teach, discipline, and attend to their children, often by training parents in basic child-rearing skills accompanied by cognitive-behavioral methods to target specific anger patterns or distorted beliefs. Similarly, treatment for child neglect focuses on parenting skills and expectations, coupled with training in social competence

TABLE 6.3 Approaches to Indicated Child Abuse Interventions

Method	Target Population	Timing of Program	Target Behaviors	Examples of Content
Parent and Family-Centered Approaches				
Child management training	Parents with serious conflict with child; parents requiring concrete demonstration and rehearsal	Early childhood; on referral to clinic	Effective parenting skills, for example, positive reinforcement, attending, commands, affect and voice tone; nonviolent discipline methods	Therapist demonstrates for parent how to use social and tangible rewards for positive child behavior
Parent education and support groups	Socially isolated; parents in need of group support, information, and sharing of feelings	Transition to parenthood; following crises or self-referral	Understanding of parental responsibilities and different approaches to child rearing; self-esteem; social skills and competence	Community resource person speaks to group about services for small children
Anger and stress management	Self- and court-referred parents demonstrating anger control problems	On recognition or admission of problem	Excessive anger, arousal, impulse control problems; inappropriate coping reactions	Parent is taught to use positive imagery or relaxation while dealing with a difficult child

Treatment of antecedent conditions in the family	Any family member(s) with major psychological or health-related problems	On recognition or admission of problem	Stress-related health problems; marital problems or violence; financial problems related to job skills, and so on	Paraprofessionals or therapists conduct marital counseling, relating to issues that affect parenting

Child-Centered Approaches

Developmental stimulation	Children showing delays in major developmental areas; parents who show inadequate stimulation	Infancy, toddlerhood, and early childhood	Expressive and receptive language; compliance; sensory-motor development; attachment	Therapist demonstrates visual, auditory, and tactile activities with child; parent imitates
Consultation with school, day care, or foster care settings	Children who may present problems across different settings and placements	On recognition; at start of new placements	Aggression, social isolation; peer problems; academic delays	Professional meets with teacher and others to suggest ways of improving child's behavior

that may include home safety, family hygiene, finances, medical needs, drug and alcohol counseling, marital counseling, and similar efforts to manage family resources and attend to children's needs (Azar & Wolfe, 1998). Although most interventions emphasize the *parent's* needs, desired changes in parenting can have a pronounced effect on their children's development as well (Wolfe & Wekerle, 1993).

Psychological characteristics of abusive parents are a good fit with behavioral methods that emphasize child-rearing and self-control skills. Behavioral strategies are concrete and problem focused and are often preferred over insight therapies among less motivated or educated clients. Interventions based on social learning theory are high in face validity and permit parents to work on problems that are most urgent and important to them. Moreover, because behavioral treatments are often perceived as more educational and problem focused, they are less threatening to families and make cooperation a bit easier to achieve (Azar & Wolfe, 1998).

Cognitive-behavioral treatment services for abusive parents typically involve some form of skills training focusing on child management skills, anger control skills, or general stress management. Training parents in effective child management skills, by far the most widely explored application of skills training, is based on practical applications of learning principles: (a) educating parents about very basic contingency management principles (e.g., reinforcement, punishment, consistency, etc.); (b) modeling for the parents (via films or live demonstrations) new ways of problem solving and increasing child compliance; (c) rehearsing the desired skills in nonthreatening situations, with increasingly more and more realistic applications (i.e., practicing in the home with the therapist); and (d) providing feedback (verbal or, in some instances, videotaped) to the parents regarding their performance of these behaviors (Wolfe, 1991). Self-control and anger control techniques have been used to reduce abusive parents' heightened arousal level and inadequate coping ability. These techniques most commonly involve several components, including the use of early detection of anger-arousal cues (e.g., physiological and/or cognitive cues), replacing anger-producing thoughts with more appropriate ones, and teaching self-control skills that would lessen the likelihood of emotional outbursts and rage (Denicola & Sandler, 1980).

A recent study illustrates some of the outcomes achieved from interventions focusing on skills and relationships. Kolko (1996) randomly assigned 55 physically abusive families to either individual child and parent cognitive-behavior therapy (CBT) or family therapy (FT). A control group received routine community services. In the CBT condition, children were provided with their own therapist who taught them ways to recognize and respond to stressful events, such as coping and self-control skills to establish safety, supports, and methods of relaxation. Parents received a separate therapist, who taught them alternatives to physical punishment using contingency management (attention, reinforcement, time-out), challenged their tendency to blame the child for not living up to their expectations, and taught them self-control skills for controlling anger and coping with stress. The FT condition was designed to enhance family functioning and relationships, to increase cooperation and motivation of all family members by promoting an understanding of coercive behavior, and to teach positive communication skills and problem solving. CBT and FT were both associated with improvements in parent-reported child behavior problems, parental distress, and family conflict and cohesion, relative to controls. Only one family in both CBT and FT showed another incident of maltreatment over a 1-year period, whereas the control group reported three incidents.

Evaluations of cognitive-behavioral approaches have been generally favorable and widely supported for several valid reasons, although knowledge of long-term outcomes is limited (Hansen, Warner-Rogers, & Hecht, 1998). These methods are effective, relative to standard protective service intervention involving brief counseling and monitoring, in modifying parental behaviors most relevant to child maltreatment, such as appropriate child-rearing and self-control skills (Wolfe, Edwards, Manion, & Koverola, 1988; Wolfe, Sandler, & Kaufman, 1981). Maltreating parents who also require very basic education and assistance in managing everyday demands, such as financial planning and home cleanliness, benefit from multicomponent interventions that address the various needs of neglectful and multiproblem families, such as marital counseling, financial planning, cleanliness, and similar concerns (Lutzker, Bigelow, Doctor, Gershater, & Greene, 1998).

Child-Focused Interventions

As noted previously, treatment services for maltreated children are less common than parent-oriented interventions largely because parental behavior is often the primary concern. Nonetheless, important strides are being made to address their developmental needs and reduce long-term impairments.

The programmatic efforts of John Fantuzzo and his colleagues provide an excellent example of a developmentally focused intervention for maltreated children. Day care activities are coupled with resilient peer treatment (RPT), a peer-mediated classroom intervention that involves pairing withdrawn children (some of whom have maltreatment histories) with resilient peers who are exceptionally strong at positive play activities (Davis & Fantuzzo,

1989; Fantuzzo, Stovall, Schachtel, Goins, & Hall, 1987; Fantuzzo et al., 1996). Play activities are specifically targeted in this program, because play is a primary means for younger children to develop peer relationship skills. Competent children are encouraged to interact with less competent children in special play areas where adults have only a minimal role. As a result, withdrawn children have the uncommon experience of being the center of another child's attention and experiencing a resilient child's repertoire of tactics for creating play and getting along with others (Fantuzzo et al., 1996). The results of this series of studies have been encouraging. Relative to controls, withdrawn children with histories of abuse or neglect show improvement in social behavior, cognitive development, self-concept, and reduction in aggressive and coercive behaviors. A further strength of this intervention is that it can be conducted in community settings, such as Head Start classrooms, that offer comprehensive services for disadvantaged children and their families (Fantuzzo et al., 1998).

CONCLUDING COMMENTS

This book has emphasized how child abuse and neglect are multiply caused phenomena that follow a recognizable pattern over the course of the developing parent-child relationship. Early patterns of parent-infant interactions that are insensitive or inadequate from an early stage can quickly transform into more power-assertive, harsh, and escalating forms of abuse or neglect. This viewpoint implies, however, that failure to deal effectively with the demands of their role early on (due to lack of resources, support, competence, or overwhelming levels of stress) can readily lead to increased pressure on the parent-child relationship and a concomitant increase in the probability of abusive behavior.

Prevention efforts tend to be organized according to specified principles that are central to their purpose, as opposed to reactions to presenting problems or urgent needs. Establishing a set of principles for designing an intervention or educational effort requires a degree of recognition and understanding of purpose that often transcends the immediate demands of the situation or population; in other words, this process relies to a large extent on adequate vision, knowledge, and planning required to entrust individuals with the skills and responsibilities they may require.

The vision for child abuse and neglect prevention captured by this analysis is one of inclusion and support, as opposed to interception and protection alone. This vision further implies that primary needs of children and families (and, by direct implication, reduction in the incidence of child abuse and neglect) are well served through supportive communities and neighborhoods. Such a vision involves diligent planning and action to ensure that communities and families receive such needed support at a point in time that is maximally beneficial (Barry, 1994).

Even among children and youth who have grown up with violence, major shifts in how they relate to others can and do happen. When such shifts from coercive to cooperative behavior do occur (and they are unfortunately the exception rather than the rule), in many cases the active ingredients involved the prominent influence of healthy, nonviolent individuals (such as teachers, foster parents, grandparents, etc.), the strength and resources of the child or youth (e.g., intelligence, good schools, and other learning opportunities), and an ambient climate of alternative, positive models and resources (Masten & Coatsworth, 1998). These are health-promoting factors that can inform efforts at prevention and early intervention.

The Long Road to Prevention

Understandably, questions and doubts arise when considering if a problem as complex as child abuse can be prevented, given how the problem cuts across many different individual, familial, and cultural issues. To be most influential, prevention-oriented approaches to child abuse must propose methods to address major high-risk factors that have been delineated throughout this book. In global terms, this purpose entails planning strategies to promote competence among parents and children, which operate in tandem with efforts to reduce the extent and type of stress faced by many families. Realistically, such a long-term vision requires that the goals and objectives be carried out progressively over many years and that they are carefully matched to family, community, and cultural interests (Melton & Barry, 1994).

Children, parents, and families who currently receive prevention services today represent an extremely diverse group, and not all benefit from such efforts. Moreover, certain key factors have not been suitably addressed to date. For example, studies have included mostly female participants, limiting the results primarily to women. Yet many risk factors identified as part of the ecological model of child maltreatment implicitly or explicitly highlight the importance of the man's role in either contributing to or preventing such events (Haskett, Marziano, & Dover, 1996). At this point in time, however, there is little information by which to design and implement services to families that will best meet the needs of men who are at risk of becoming violent toward children or partners. This finding of underrepresentation of fathers compared with mothers is consistent with the literature on developmental psychopathology in general. Despite the growing knowledge that fathers play a significant role in the development of child and adolescent problems and in the etiology of physical and sexual abuse (Phares & Compas, 1992), intervention programs have generally not included men in their programs.

A further roadblock to prevention is that due to limited resources and urgent demands, many communities are being forced to evolve into a pattern of crisis management in response to child and family needs. Child welfare laws are designed solely for protection, which often translates into service providers being forced to wait, or for families to remain undetected, until it is absolutely necessary before making any attempt at intervention or reform. Persons who work with troubled children or at-risk parents, unfortunately, often are left with a task that is beyond the capabilities of the current system and resources—too little, too late—resulting in the well-known signs of stress and job turnover.

A conceptual shift is gradually occurring that acknowledges the contribution of each member of society and the benefits of participatory (in contrast to mandatory) involvement. An emerging perspective throughout the health and mental health fields emphasizes health promotion and empowerment, by encouraging new changes, opportunities, and competence to achieve one's health potential (Millstein, Petersen, & Nightingale, 1993). A health promotion perspective speaks to the importance of attaining a balance between the abilities of the individual (or groups of individuals) and the challenges and risks of the environment (Wallerstein, 1992).

The prevention of child abuse, in the final analysis, should encourage diversity and opportunities for the development of unique resources among children and parents. Societal influences that play a role in child abuse and neglect, especially in circumstances where families are exposed to major effects of poverty, health risks, and environmental conflict, require more concerted efforts. The special risks and strengths of diverse cultural and ethnic groups need to be addressed, along with greater sensitivity to ethnic and cultural issues in the planning of services. Such a cross-cultural perspective to child abuse and neglect intervention and prevention would redirect the focus away from individuals and families and explore societal and cultural conditions that attenuate or exacerbate these problems (Sipes, 1992).

REFERENCES

Aber, J. L., Allen, J., Carlson, V., & Cicchetti, D. (1989). The effects of maltreatment on development during early childhood: Recent studies and their theoretical, clinical, and policy implications. In D. Cicchetti & V. Carlson (Eds.), *Child maltreatment: Theory and research on the causes and consequences of child abuse and neglect* (pp. 579-619). New York: Cambridge University Press.

Aber, J. L., & Cicchetti, D. (1984). The socio-emotional development of maltreated children: An empirical and theoretical analysis. In H. Fitzgerald, B. Lester, & M. Yogman (Eds.), *Theory and research in behavioral pediatrics* (Vol 2., pp. 147-199). New York: Plenum.

Achenbach, T. M. (1990). Conceptualization of developmental psychopathology. In M. Lewis & S. M. Miller (Eds.), *Handbook of developmental psychopathology* (pp. 3-14). New York: Plenum.

Albee, G. (1985). The argument for primary prevention. *Journal of Primary Prevention, 5,* 213-219.

Alessandri, S. M., & Lewis, M. (1996). Differences in pride and shame in maltreated and nonmaltreated preschoolers. *Child Development, 67,* 1857-1869.

Allen, D. M., & Tarnowski, K. J. (1989). Depressive characteristics of physically abused children. *Journal of Abnormal Child Psychology, 17,* 1-11.

American Association for Protecting Children. (1988). *Highlights of official child neglect and abuse reporting, 1986.* Denver: American Humane Association.

American Humane Association. (1984). *Trends in child abuse and neglect: A national perspective.* Denver, CO: Author.

American Psychological Association. (1996). *Presidential Task Force on Violence and the Family.* Washington, DC: Author.

Ammerman, R. T., & Patz, R. J. (1996). Determinants of child abuse potential: Contributions of parent and child factors. *Journal of Clinical Child Psychology, 25,* 300-307.

Aronen, E. T., & Kurkela, S. A. (1996). Long-term effects of an early home-based intervention. *Journal of the American Academy of Child and Adolescent Psychiatry, 35* (12), 1665-1672.

Averill, J. R. (1983). Studies on anger and aggression: Implications for theories of emotion. *American Psychologist, 38,* 1145-1160.

Azar, S. T. (1991). Models of physical child abuse: A metatheoretical analysis. *Criminal Justice and Behavior, 18,* 30-46.

Azar, S. T. (1997). A cognitive behavioral approach to understanding and treating parents who physically abuse their children. In D. A. Wolfe, R. J. McMahon, & R. Dev

Peters (Eds.), *Child abuse: New directions in prevention and treatment across the lifespan* (pp. 78-100). Thousand Oaks, CA: Sage.

Azar, S. T., Barnes, K. T., & Twentyman, C. T. (1988). Developmental outcomes in physically abused children: Consequences of parental abuse or the effects of a more general breakdown in caregiving behaviors? *The Behavior Therapist, 11,* 27-32.

Azar, S. T., Robinson, D. R., Hekimian, E., & Twentyman, C. T. (1984). Unrealistic expectations and problem-solving ability in maltreating and comparison mothers. *Journal of Consulting and Clinical Psychology, 52,* 687-691.

Azar, S., & Wolfe, D. (1998). Child physical abuse and neglect. In E. J. Mash & R. A. Barkley (Eds.), *Treatment of childhood disorders* (2nd ed., pp. 501-544). New York: Guilford.

Bandura, A. (1973). *Aggression: A social learning analysis.* Englewood Cliffs, NJ: Prentice Hall.

Barahal, R. M., Waterman, J., & Martin, H. P. (1981). The social cognitive development of abused children. *Journal of Consulting and Clinical Psychology, 49,* 508-516.

Barry, F. (1994). A neighborhood-based approach: What is it? In G. B. Melton & F. D. Barry (Eds.), *Protecting children from abuse and neglect: Foundations for a new national strategy* (pp. 14-39). New York: Guilford.

Bauer, W. D., & Twentyman, C. T. (1985). Abusing, neglectful, and comparison mothers' responses to child-related and non-child-related stressors. *Journal of Consulting and Clinical Psychology, 53,* 335-343.

Baumrind, D. (1971). Current patterns of parental authority. *Developmental Psychology Monographs, 4* (1, Pt. 2).

Baumrind, D., & Black, A. E. (1967). Socialization practices associated with dimensions of competence in preschool boys and girls. *Child Development, 38,* 291-327.

Becker, J. V., Alpert, J. L., BigFoot, D. S., Bonner, B. L., Geddie, L. F., Henggeler, S. W., Kaufman, K. L., & Walker, C. E. (1995). Empirical research on child abuse treatment: Report by the Child Abuse and Neglect Treatment Working Group, American Psychological Association. *Journal of Clinical Child Psychology, 24,* 23-46.

Beeghly, M., & Cicchetti, D. (1994). Child maltreatment, attachment, and the self system: Emergence of an internal state lexicon in toddlers at high social risk. *Development and Psychopathology, 6,* 5-30.

Bell, G. (1973). Parents who abuse their children. *Canadian Psychiatric Association Journal, 18,* 223-228.

Bell, R. Q., & Harper, L. (1977). *Child effects on adults.* Hillsdale, NJ: Lawrence Erlbaum.

Belsky, J. (1980). Child maltreatment: An ecological integration. *American Psychologist, 35,* 320-335.

Belsky, J. (1984). The determinants of parenting: A process model. *Child Development, 55,* 83-96.

Berkowitz, L. (1983). Aversively stimulated aggression: Some parallels and differences in research with animals and humans. *American Psychologist, 38,* 1135-1144.

Bernstein, D. P., Fink, L., Handelsman, L., Foote, J., Lovejoy, M., Wenzel, K., Sapareto, E., & Ruggiero, J. (1994). Initial reliability and validity of a new retrospective measure of child abuse and neglect. *American Journal of Psychiatry, 151,* 1132-1136.

Besharov, D. J. (1982). Toward better research on child abuse and neglect: Making definitional issues an explicit methodological concern. *Child Abuse & Neglect, 5,* 383-390.

Birns, B., Cascardi, M., & Meyer, S. (1990). Sex-role socialization: Developmental influences on wife abuse. *American Journal of Orthopsychiatry, 64,* 50-59.

Blumberg, M. L. (1974). Psychopathology of the abusing parent. *American Journal of Psychotherapy, 28,* 21-29.

Bousha, D. M., & Twentyman, C. T. (1984). Mother-child interactional style in abuse, neglect, and control groups: Naturalistic observations in the home. *Journal of Abnormal Psychology, 93,* 106-114.

Bower, G. H. (1981). Mood and memory. *American Psychologist, 36,* 129-148.

Bretherton, I., Fritz, J., Zahn-Waxler, C., & Ridgeway, D. (1986). Learning to talk about emotions: A functionalist perspective. *Child Development, 57,* 529-548.

Britner, P. A., & Reppucci, N. D. (1997). Prevention of child maltreatment: Evaluation of a parent education program for teen mothers. *Journal of Child and Family Studies, 6,* 165-175.

Broadbent, A., & Bentley, R. (1997). *Child abuse and neglect Australia 1995-96* (Child Welfare Series, No. 17; AIHW Cat. No. CWS 1). Canberra: Australian Institute of Health and Welfare.

Bronfenbrenner, U. (1977). Toward an experimental ecology of human development. *American Psychologist, 52,* 513-531.

Brooks-Gunn, J., & Duncan, G. J. (1997). The effects of poverty on children. *The Future of Children, 7*(2), 55-71.

Bross, D. C. (1997). The legal context of child abuse and neglect: Balancing the rights of children and parents in a demographic society. In M. E. Helfer, R. S. Kempe, & R. D. Krugman (Eds.), *The battered child* (5th ed., pp. 61-72). Chicago: University of Chicago Press.

Brown, G. W., & Harris, T. (1978). *Social origins of depression: A study of psychiatric disorder in women.* London: Tavistock.

Browne, A., & Finkelhor, D. (1986). Impact of child sexual abuse: A review of the literature. *Psychological Bulletin, 99,* 66-77.

Bugental, D. B. (1993). Communication in abusive relationships: Cognitive constructions of interpersonal power. *American Behavioral Scientist, 36,* 288-308.

Bugental, D. B., Blue, J., & Lewis, J. (1990). Caregiver beliefs and dysphoric affect to difficult children. *Developmental Psychology, 26,* 631-638.

Bugental, D. B., & Shennum, W. A. (1984). "Difficult" children as elicitors and targets of adult communication patterns: An attributional-behavioral transactional analysis. *Monographs for the Society for Research in Child Development, 49* (1, Serial No. 205).

Burgess, R. L. (1985). Social incompetence as a precipitant to and consequence of child maltreatment. *Victomology: An International Journal, 10,* 72-86.

Burgess, R. L., & Conger, R. (1978). Family interactions in abusive, neglectful, and normal families. *Child Development, 49,* 1163-1173.

Burgess, R. L., & Youngblade, L. M. (1988). Social incompetence and the intergenerational transmission of abusive parental practices. In G. T. Hotaling, D. Finkelhor, J. T. Kirkpatrick, & M. A. Straus (Eds.), *Family abuse and its consequences: New directions in research* (pp. 38-60). Newbury Park, CA: Sage.

Burhans, K. K., & Dweck, C. S. (1995). Helplessness in early childhood: The role of contingent worth. *Child Development, 66,* 1719-1738.

Caffey, J. (1946). Multiple fractures in the long bones of infants suffering from chronic subdural hematoma. *American Journal of Roentgenology, 56,* 163-173.

Caplan, P. J., & Dinardo, L. (1986). Is there a relationship between child abuse and learning disability? *Canadian Journal of Behavioural Sciences, 18,* 367-380.

Carlson, E. A., & Sroufe, L. A. (1995). Contribution of attachment theory to developmental psychopathology. In D. Cicchetti & D. J. Cohen (Eds.), *Developmental psychopathology: Vol. 1. Theory and Methods* (pp. 581-617). New York: John Wiley.

Carlson, V., Cicchetti, D., Barnett, D., & Braunwald, K. (1989). Finding order in disorganization: Lesson from research on maltreated infants' attachments to their caregivers. In D. Cicchetti & V. Carlson (Eds.), *Child maltreatment: Theory and research on the causes and consequences of child abuse and neglect* (pp. 494-528). New York: Cambridge University Press.

Center on Child Abuse Prevention Research. (1996). *Intensive home visitation: A trial, follow-up, and risk assessment study of Hawaii's health start program.* Chicago: National Committee to Prevent Child Abuse.

Chaffin, M., Kelleher, K., & Hollenberg, J. (1996). Onset of physical abuse and neglect: Psychiatric, substance abuse, and social risk factors from prospective community data. *Child Abuse & Neglect, 20,* 191-203.

Cicchetti, D. (1990). The organization and coherence of socioemotional, cognitive, and representational development: Illustrations through a developmental psychopathology perspective on Down syndrome and child maltreatment. In R. Thompson (Ed.), *Nebraska Symposium on Motivation: Vol. 36. Socioemotional development* (pp. 259-366). Lincoln: University of Nebraska Press.

Cicchetti, D., & Beeghly, M. (1987). Symbolic development in maltreated youngsters: An organizational perspective. *New Directions for Child Development, 36,* 5-29.

Cicchetti, D., Ganiban, J., & Barnett, D. (1990). Contributions from the study of high risk populations to understanding the development of emotion regulation. In K. Dodge & J. Garber (Eds.), *The development of emotion regulation* (pp. 1-54). New York: Cambridge University Press.

Cicchetti, D., & Lynch, M. (1995). Failures in the expectable environment and their impact on individual development: The case of child maltreatment. In D. Cicchetti & D. J. Cohen (Eds.), *Developmental psychopathology: Vol. 2. Risk, disorder, and adaptation* (pp. 32-71). New York: John Wiley.

Cicchetti, D., & Olsen, K. (1990). The developmental psychopathology of child maltreatment. In M. Lewis & S. M. Miller (Eds.), *Handbook of developmental psychopathology* (pp. 261-279). New York: Plenum.

Cicchetti, D., & Richters, J. E. (1993). Developmental considerations in the investigation of conduct disorder. *Development and Psychopathology, 5,* 331-344.

Cicchetti, D., & Rizley, R. (1981). Developmental perspectives on the etiology, intergenerational transmission, and sequelae of child maltreatment. In D. Cicchetti & R. Rizley (Eds.), *New directions for child development: Developmental perspectives on child maltreatment* (pp. 31-55). San Francisco: Jossey-Bass.

Cicchetti, D., & Rogosch, F. A. (1997). The role of self-organization in the promotion of resilience in maltreated children. *Development and Psychopathology, 9,* 797-815.

Cicchetti, D., Toth, S., & Bush, M. (1988). Developmental psychopathology and incompetence in childhood: Suggestions for intervention. In B. B. Lahey & A. E. Kazdin

(Eds.), *Advances in clinical child psychology* (Vol. 11, pp. 1-77). New York: Plenum.

Claussen, A. K., & Crittenden, P. M. (1991). Physical and psychological maltreatment: Relations among types of maltreatment. *Child Abuse & Neglect, 15,* 5-18.

Conger, R. D., Burgess, R., & Barrett, C. (1979). Child abuse related to life change and perceptions of illness: Some preliminary findings. *Family Coordinator, 28,* 73-78.

Coohey, C. (1996). Child maltreatment: Testing the social isolation hypothesis. *Child Abuse & Neglect, 20,* 241-254.

Coopersmith, S. (1967). *The antecedents of self-esteem.* San Francisco: W. H. Freeman.

Corcoran, M. E., & Chaudry, A. (1997). The dynamics of childhood poverty. *The Future of Children, 7*(2), 40-54.

Coster, W., & Cicchetti, D. (1993). Research on the communicative development of maltreated children: Clinical implications. *Topics in Language Disorders, 13*(4), 25-38.

Coulton, C. J., Korbin, J. E., Su, M., & Chow, J. (1995). Community level factors and child maltreatment rates. *Child Development, 66,* 1262-1276.

Crittenden, P. (1988). Relationships at risk. In J. Belsky & T. Nezworski (Eds.), *Clinical implications of attachment theory* (pp. 136-174). Hillsdale, NJ: Lawrence Erlbaum.

Crittenden, P. M. (1992). Quality of attachment in the preschool years. *Development and Psychopathology, 4,* 209-241.

Crittenden, P. M. (1993). An information-processing perspective on the behavior of neglectful parents. *Criminal Justice and Behavior, 20,* 27-48.

Crittenden, P. M., & Ainsworth, M. (1989). Attachment and child abuse. In D. Cicchetti & V. Carlson (Eds.), *Child maltreatment: Theory and research on the causes and consequences of child abuse and neglect* (pp. 432-463). New York: Cambridge University Press.

Crittenden, P. M., & Bonvillian, J. D. (1984). The relationship between maternal risk status and maternal sensitivity. *American Journal of Orthopsychiatry, 54,* 250-262.

Crittenden, P., & DiLalla, D. L. (1988). Compulsive compliance: The development of an inhibitory coping strategy in infancy. *Journal of Abnormal Child Psychology, 16,* 585-599.

Cummings, E. M. (1997). Marital conflict, abuse, and adversity in the family and child adjustment: A developmental psychopathology perspective. In D. A. Wolfe, R. J. McMahon, & R. Dev Peters (Eds.), *Child abuse: New directions in prevention and treatment across the lifespan* (pp. 1-24). Thousand Oaks, CA: Sage.

Daro, D., & Harding, K. (in press). Healthy Families America: Using research to enhance practice. *The Future of Children.*

Davis, S., & Fantuzzo, J. W. (1989). The effects of adult and peer social initiations on social behavior of withdrawn and aggressive maltreated preschool children. *Journal of Family Violence, 4,* 227-248.

Denicola, J., & Sandler, J. (1980). Training abusive parents in child management and self-control skills. *Behavior Therapy, 11,* 263-270.

Dietrich, K. N., Starr, R. H., & Kaplan, M. G. (1980). Maternal stimulation and care of abused infants. In T. M. Field, S. Goldberg, D. Stern, & A. M. Sostek (Eds.), *High-risk infants and children: Adult and peer interactions* (pp. 25-41). New York: Academic Press.

Disbrow, M. A., Doerr, H., & Caulfield, C. (1977). Measuring the components of parents' potential for child abuse and neglect. *Child Abuse & Neglect, 1,* 279-296.

Dodge, K. A., Bates, J. E., & Pettit, G. S. (1990). Mechanisms in the cycle of violence. *Science, 250,* 1678-1682.

Dodge, K. A., Pettit, G. S., & Bates, J. E. (1994). Effects of physical maltreatment on the development of peer relations. *Development and Psychopathology, 6,* 43-55.

Downey, G., & Walker, E. (1992). Distinguishing family-level and child-level influences on the development of depression and aggression in children at risk. *Development and Psychopathology, 4,* 81-95.

Drake, B., & Pandey, S. (1996). Understanding the relationship between neighborhood poverty and specific types of child maltreatment. *Child Abuse & Neglect, 20,* 1003-1018.

Dumas, J., & Wahler, R. G. (1985). Indiscriminate mothering as a contextual factor in aggressive-oppositional child behavior: "Damned if you do, damned if you don't." *Journal of Abnormal Child Psychology, 13,* 1-17.

Duncan, R. D., Saunders, B. E., Kilpatrick, D. G., Hanson, R. F., & Resnick, H. S. (1996). Childhood physical assault as a risk factor for PTSD, depression, and substance abuse: Findings from a national survey. *American Journal of Orthopsychiatry, 66,* 437-448.

During, S. M., & McMahon, R. J. (1991). Recognition of emotional facial expressions by abusive mothers and their children. *Journal of Clinical Child Psychology, 20*(2), 132-139.

Eckenrode, J., Laird, M., & Doris, J. (1993). School performance and disciplinary problems among abused and neglected children. *Developmental Psychology, 29,* 53-62.

Eckenrode, J., Rowe, E., Laird, M., & Brathwaite, J. (1995). Mobility as a mediator of the effects of child maltreatment on academic performance. *Child Development, 66,* 1130-1142.

Edleson, J. L. (1999). The overlap between child maltreatment and woman battering. *Violence Against Women, 5,* 134-154.

Edleson, J. L., Eisikovits, Z. C., Guttmann, E., & Sela-Amit, M. (1991). Cognitive and interpersonal factors in woman abuse. *Journal of Family Violence, 6,* 167-182.

Egeland, B., Breitenbucher, M., & Rosenberg, D. (1980). Prospective study of the significance of life stress in the etiology of child abuse. *Journal of Consulting and Clinical Psychology, 48,* 195-205.

Egeland, B., & Farber, E. A. (1984). Infant-mother attachment: Factors related to its development and changes over time. *Child Development, 55,* 753-771.

Egeland, B., & Sroufe, L. A. (1981). Attachment and early maltreatment. *Child Development, 52,* 44-52.

Egeland, B., & Vaughn, B. (1981). Failure of "bond formation" as a cause of abuse, neglect, and maltreatment. *American Journal of Orthopsychiatry, 51,* 78-84.

Elmer, E. (1963). Identification of abused children. *Children, 10,* 180-184.

Erickson, M., Egeland, B., & Pianta, R. (1989). The effects of maltreatment on the development of young children. In D. Cicchetti & V. Carlson (Eds.), *Child maltreatment: Theory and research on the causes and consequences of child abuse and neglect* (pp. 647-684). New York: Cambridge University Press.

Fantuzzo, J. W., Stovall, A., Schachtel, D., Goins, C., & Hall, R. (1987). The effects of peer social initiations on the social behavior of withdrawn maltreated preschool children. *Journal of Behavior Therapy and Experimental Psychiatry, 4,* 357-363.

Fantuzzo, J., Sutton-Smith, B., Atkins, M., Meyers, R., Stevenson, H., Coolahan, K., Weiss, A., & Manz, P. (1996). Community-based resilient peer treatment of withdrawn maltreated preschool children. *Journal of Consulting and Clinical Psychology, 64,* 1377-1386.

Fantuzzo, J., Weiss, A. D., & Coolahan, K. C. (1998). Community-based partnership-directed research: Actualizing community strengths to treat child victims of physical abuse and neglect. In J. R. Lutzker (Ed.), *Handbook of child abuse research and treatment* (pp. 213-237). New York: Plenum.

Feldman, C. M. (1997). Childhood precursors of adult interpersonal violence. *Clinical Psychology: Science and Practice, 4,* 307-334.

Feldman, R. S., Salzinger, S., Rosario, M., Alvarado, L., Caraballo, L., & Hammer, M. (1995). Parent, teacher, and peer ratings of physically abused and nonmaltreated children's behavior. *Journal of Abnormal Child Psychology, 23,* 317-334.

Feshbach, S. (1980). Child abuse and the dynamics of human aggression and violence. In G. Gerbner, C. J. Ross, & E. Zigler (Eds.), *Child abuse: An agenda for action* (pp. 48-60). New York: Oxford University Press.

Fincham, F. D., Bradbury, T. N., & Grych, J. H. (1990). Conflict in close relationships: The role of intrapersonal phenomena. In S. Graham & V. S. Folkes (Eds.), *Attribution theory: Applications to achievement, mental health, and interpersonal conflict* (pp. 161-184). Hillsdale, NJ: Lawrence Erlbaum.

Finkelhor, D. (1993). Epidemiological factors in the clinical identification of child sexual abuse. *Child Abuse & Neglect, 17,* 67-70.

Finkelhor, D. (1994). The international epidemiology of child sexual abuse. *Child Abuse & Neglect, 18,* 409-417.

Finkelhor, D. (1995). The victimization of children: A developmental perspective. *American Journal of Orthopsychiatry, 65,* 177-193.

Finkelhor, D., & Browne, A. (1988). Assessing the long-term impact of child sexual abuse: A review and conceptualization. In L. Walker (Ed.), *Handbook on sexual abuse of children* (pp. 55-71). New York: Springer.

Flisher, A. J., Kramer, R. A., Hoven, C. W., Greenwald, S., Alegria, M., Bird, H. R., Canino, G., Connell, R., & Moore, R. E. (1997). Psychosocial characteristics of physically abused children and adolescents. *Journal of the American Academy of Child and Adolescent Psychiatry, 36,* 123-131.

Folkman, S. (1984). Personal control and stress and coping processes: A transactional analysis. *Journal of Personality and Social Psychology, 46,* 839-852.

Friedman, R., Sandler, J., Hernandez, M., & Wolfe, D. (1981). Child abuse. In E. Mash & L. Terdal (Eds.), *Behavioral assessment of childhood disorders* (pp. 221-255). New York: Guilford.

Friedrich, W. N. (1990). *Psychotherapy of sexually abused children and their families.* New York: W. W. Norton.

Friedrich, W. N., Jaworski, T. M., Huxsahl, J. E., & Bengston, B. S. (1997). Dissociative and sexual behaviors in children and adolescents with sexual abuse and psychiatric histories. *Journal of Interpersonal Violence, 12*(2), 155-171.

Frodi, A. M., & Lamb, M. E. (1980). Child abusers' responses to infant smiles and cries. *Child Development, 51,* 238-241.

Frodi, A. M., & Smetana, J. (1984). Abused, neglected, and nonmaltreated preschoolers' ability to discriminate emotions in others: The effects of IQ. *Child Abuse & Neglect, 8,* 459-465.

Gaensbauer, T. J., & Sands, K. (1979). Distorted affective communication in abused/neglected infants and their potential impact on caretakers. *Journal of the American Academy of Child Psychiatry, 18,* 236-250.

Gaines, R., Sandgrund, A., Green, A. H., & Power, E. (1978). Etiological factors in child maltreatment: A multivariate study of abusing, neglecting, and normal mothers. *Journal of Abnormal Psychology, 87,* 531-540.

Gallup Organization. (1995). *Disciplining children in America: A Gallup poll report.* Princeton, NJ: Author.

Garbarino, J. (1976). A preliminary study of some ecological correlates of child abuse: The impact of socioeconomic stress on mothers. *Child Development, 47,* 178-185.

Garbarino, J. (1977). The human ecology of child maltreatment: A conceptual model for research. *Journal of Marriage and the Family, 39,* 721-735.

Garbarino, J. (1997). The role of economic deprivation in the social context of child maltreatment. In M. E. Helfer, R. S. Kempe, & R. D. Krugman (Eds.), *The battered child* (5th ed., pp. 49-60). Chicago: University of Chicago Press.

Garbarino, J., Guttman, E., & Seeley, J. (1986). *The psychologically battered child.* San Francisco: Jossey-Bass.

Garbarino, J., & Stocking, S. H. (1980). *Protecting children from abuse and neglect.* San Francisco: Jossey-Bass.

Garmezy, N. (1983). Stressors of childhood. In N. Garmezy & M. Rutter (Eds.), *Stress, coping, and development in children* (pp. 43-84). New York: McGraw-Hill.

Gelles, R. J. (1973). Child abuse as psychopathology: A sociological critique and reformulation. *American Journal of Orthopsychiatry, 43,* 611-621.

Gelles, R. J. (1983). An exchange/social control theory. In D. Finkelhor, R. J. Gelles, G. T. Hotaling, & M. A. Straus (Eds.), *The dark side of families* (pp. 151-165). Beverly Hills, CA: Sage.

George, C., & Main, M. (1979). Social interactions of young abused children: Approach, avoidance, and aggression. *Child Development, 50,* 306-318.

Gil, D. G. (1970). *Violence against children: Physical child abuse in the United States.* Cambridge, MA: Harvard University Press.

Giovannoni, J. M., & Becerra, R. M. (1979). *Defining child abuse.* New York: Free Press.

Gordon, R. S. (1983). An operational classification of disease prevention. *Public Health Reports, 98,* 107-109.

Green, A. H. (1976). A psychodynamic approach to the study and treatment of child-abusing parents. *Journal of the American Academy of Child Psychiatry, 15,* 414-429.

Green, A. H., Gaines, R. W., & Sandgrund, A. (1974). Child abuse: Pathological syndrome of family interaction. *American Journal of Psychiatry, 131,* 882-886.

Hansen, D. J., Warner-Rogers, J. E., & Hecht, D. B. (1998). Implementing and evaluating an individualized behavioral intervention program for maltreating families. In J. R. Lutzker (Ed.), *Handbook of child abuse research and treatment* (pp. 133-158). New York: Plenum.

Harrington, D., Dubowitz, H., Black, M. M., & Binder, A. (1995). Maternal substance use and neglectful parenting: Relations with children's development. *Journal of Clinical Child Psychology, 24,* 258-263.

Hartman C. R., & Burgess, A. W. (1989). Sexual abuse of children: Causes and consequences. In D. Cicchetti & V. Carlson (Eds.), *Child maltreatment: Theory and research on the causes and consequences of child abuse and neglect* (pp. 95-128). Cambridge, UK: Cambridge University Press.

Haskett, M. E., & Kistner, J. A. (1991). Social interactions and peer perceptions of young physically abused children. *Child Development, 62,* 979-990.

Haskett, M. E., Marziano, B., & Dover, E. R. (1996). Absence of males in maltreatment research: A survey of recent literature. *Child Abuse & Neglect, 20,* 1175-1182.

Hazzard, A., Celano, M., Gould, J., Lawry, S., & Webb, C. (1995). Predicting symptomatology and self-blame among child sex abuse victims. *Child Abuse & Neglect, 19,* 707-714.

Helfer, R. E. (1973). The etiology of child abuse. *Pediatrics, 51,* 777.

Henderson, A. S., & Moran, P. A. P. (1983). Social relationships during the onset and remission of neurotic symptoms: A prospective community study. *British Journal of Psychiatry, 143,* 467-472.

Hennessy, K. D., Rabideau, G. J., Cicchetti, D., & Cummings, E. M. (1994). Responses of physically abused children to different forms of interadult anger. *Child Development, 65,* 815-828.

Herman, J. L. (1992). *Trauma and recovery: The aftermath of violence—From domestic abuse to political terror.* New York: Basic Books.

Herrenkohl, E. C., Herrenkohl, R. C., Toedter, L., & Yanushefski, A. M. (1984). Parent-child interactions in abusive and non-abusive families. *Journal of the American Academy of Child Psychiatry, 23,* 641-648.

Herrenkohl, R. C., Herrenkohl, E. C., & Egolf, B. P. (1983). Circumstances surrounding the occurrence of child maltreatment. *Journal of Consulting and Clinical Psychology, 51,* 424-431.

Hillson, J. M. C., & Kuiper, N. A. (1994). A stress and coping model of child maltreatment. *Clinical Psychology Review, 14,* 261-285.

Hilton, N. Z. (1992). Battered women's concerns about their children witnessing wife assault. *Journal of Interpersonal Violence, 7,* 77-86.

Hoffman, M. L. (1970). Moral development. In P. H. Mussen (Ed.), *Carmichael's manual of child psychology* (Vol. 2, pp. 261-359). New York: John Wiley.

Hoffman, M. L. (1975). Moral internalization, parental power and the nature of parent-child internalization. *Developmental Psychology, 11,* 228-239.

Hoffman-Plotkin, D., & Twentyman, C. T. (1984). A multimodal assessment of behavioral and cognitive deficits in abused and neglected preschoolers. *Child Development, 55,* 794-802.

Institute of Medicine. (1989). *Research on children and adolescents with mental, behavioral and developmental disorders.* Washington, DC: National Academy Press.

Jacobson, N. S., Gottman, J. M., Waltz, J., Rushe, R., Babcock, J., & Holtzworth-Munroe, A. (1994). Affect, verbal content, and psychophysiology in the arguments of couples with a violent husband. *Journal of Consulting and Clinical Psychology, 62,* 982-988.

Jaffe, P., Lemon, N., Sandler, J., & Wolfe, D. (1996). *Working together to end domestic violence.* Tampa, FL: Mancorp.

Jaffe, P., Wolfe, D. A., & Wilson, S. (1990). *Children of battered women.* Newbury Park, CA: Sage.

Jessor, R. (1993). Successful adolescent development among youth in high-risk settings. *American Psychologist, 48,* 117-126.

Kadushin, A., & Martin, J. A. (1981). *Child abuse: An interactional event.* New York: Columbia University Press.

Kagan, J. (1983). Stress and coping in early development. In N. Garmezy & M. Rutter (Eds.), *Stress, coping, and development in children* (pp. 191-216). New York: McGraw-Hill.

Kaplan, F. K., Eichler, L. S., & Winickoff, S. A. (1980). *Pregnancy, birth, and parenthood.* San Francisco: Jossey-Bass.

Kaufman, J. L. (1991). Depressive disorders in maltreated children. *American Journal of Child and Adolescent Psychiatry, 30,* 257-265.

Kaufman, J. L., & Zigler, E. (1989). The intergenerational transmission of child abuse. In D. Cicchetti & V. Carlson (Eds.), *Child maltreatment: Theory and research on the causes and consequences of child abuse and neglect* (pp. 129-150). New York: Cambridge University Press.

Kazdin, A. E., Moser, J., Colbus, D., & Bell, R. (1985). Depressive symptoms among physically abused and psychiatrically disturbed children. *Journal of Abnormal Psychology, 94,* 298-307.

Kelleher, K., Chaffin, M., Hollenberg, J., & Fischer, E. (1994). Alcohol and drug disorders among physically abusive and neglectful parents in a community-based sample. *American Journal of Public Health, 84,* 1586-1590.

Kempe, C. H., & Helfer, R. E. (1972). *Helping the battered child and his family.* Philadelphia: J. B. Lippincott.

Kempe, C. H., Silverman, F. N., Steele, B. F., Droegemueller, W., & Silver, H. K. (1962). The battered child syndrome. *Journal of the American Medical Association, 181,* 17-24.

Kendall, P. C. (1993). Cognitive-behavioral therapies with youth: Guiding theory, current status, and emerging developments. *Journal of Consulting and Clinical Psychology, 61,* 235-247.

Kendall-Tackett, K. A., Williams, L. M., & Finkelhor, D. (1993). The impact of sexual abuse on children: A review and synthesis of recent empirical studies. *Psychological Bulletin, 113,* 164-180.

Kinard, E. M. (1980). Emotional development in physically abused children. *American Journal of Orthopsychiatry, 50,* 686-696.

Kinard, E. M. (1995). Perceived social support and competence in abused children: A longitudinal perspective. *Journal of Family Violence, 10,* 73-98.

Knutson, J. F. (1978). Child abuse as an area of aggression research. *Journal of Pediatric Psychology, 3,* 20-27.

Knutson, J. F., & Bower, M. E. (1994). Physically abusive parenting as an escalated aggressive response. In M. Potegal & J. F. Knutson (Eds.), *The dynamics of aggression: Biological and social processes in dyads and groups* (pp. 195-225). Hillsdale, NJ: Lawrence Erlbaum.

Kolko, D. J. (1992). Characteristics of child victims of physical violence: Research findings and clinical implications. *Journal of Interpersonal Violence, 7,* 244-276.

Kolko, D. J. (1996). Individual cognitive behavioral treatment and family therapy for physically abused children and their offending parents: A comparison of clinical outcomes. *Child Maltreatment, 1,* 322-342.

Korbin, J. (1994). Sociocultural factors in child maltreatment. In G. B. Melton & F. D. Barry (Eds.), *Protecting children from abuse and neglect: Foundations for a new national strategy* (pp. 182-223). New York: Guilford.

Koverola, C., Pound, J., Heger, A., & Lytle, C. (1993). Relationship of child sexual abuse to depression. *Child Abuse & Neglect, 17,* 393-400.

Kurtz, P. D., Gaudin, J. M., Jr., Wodarski, J. S., & Howing, P. T. (1993). Maltreatment and the school-aged child: School performance consequences. *Child Abuse & Neglect, 17,* 581-589.

Lahey, B. B., Conger, R. D., Atkeson, B. M., & Treiber, F. A. (1984). Parenting behavior and emotional status of physically abusive mothers. *Journal of Consulting and Clinical Psychology, 52,* 1062-1071.

LaRose, L., & Wolfe, D. A. (1987). Psychological characteristics of parents who abuse or neglect their children. In B. B. Lahey & A. E. Kazdin (Eds.), *Advances in Clinical Child Psychology* (Vol. 10, pp. 55-97). New York: Plenum.

Larrance, D. T., & Twentyman, C. T. (1983). Maternal attributions and child abuse. *Journal of Abnormal Psychology, 92,* 449-457.

Lazarus, R. S. (1981). The stress and coping paradigm. In C. Eisdoefer, D. Cohen, A. Kleinamn, & P. Maxim (Eds.), *Models for clinical psychopathology* (pp. 177-214). New York: Spectrum.

Lefcourt, H. M. (1973). The function of the illusions of control and freedom. *American Psychologist, 28,* 417-425.

Leventhal, J. (1997). The prevention of child abuse and neglect: Pipe dreams of possibilities? *Clinical Child Psychology and Psychiatry, 2,* 489-500.

Levine, S. (1983). A psychobiological approach to the ontogeny of coping. In N. Garmezy & M. Rutter (Eds.), *Stress, coping, and development in children* (pp. 107-131). New York: McGraw-Hill.

Lewis, D. O., Pincus, J. H., & Glaser, G. H. (1979). Violent juvenile delinquents: Psychiatric, neurological, psychological, and abuse factors. *Journal of the American Academy of Child Psychiatry, 18,* 307-319.

Lewis, M. (1990). Models of developmental psychopathology. In M. Lewis & S. M. Miller (Eds.), *Handbook of developmental psychopathology* (pp. 15-27). New York: Plenum.

Lewis, M. (1992). *Shame: The exposed self.* New York: Free Press.

Light, R. (1973). Abused and neglected children in America: A study of alternative policies. *Harvard Educational Review, 43,* 556-598.

Loeber, R. (1991). Questions and advances in the study of developmental pathways. In D. Cicchetti & S. L. Toth (Eds.), *Rochester symposium on developmental psychopathology: Vol. 3. Models and integrations* (pp. 97-116). Rochester, NY: University of Rochester Press.

Loeber, R., Weissman, W., & Reid, J. (1983). Family interactions of assaultive adolescents, stealers, and nondelinquents. *Journal of Abnormal Child Psychology, 11,* 1-14.

Lorber, R., Felton, D. K., & Reid, J. (1984). A social learning approach to the reduction of coercive processes in child abusive families: A molecular analysis. *Advances in Behavior Research and Therapy, 6,* 29-45.

Lorion, R. P., Myers, T. G., Bartels, C., & Dennis, A. (1994). Preventive intervention research: Pathways for extending knowledge of child/adolescent health and pathology. In T. H. Ollendick & R. J. Prinz (Eds.), *Advances in clinical child psychology* (Vol. 16, pp. 109-139). New York: Plenum.

Luntz, B. K., & Widom, C. S. (1994). Antisocial personality disorder in abused and neglected children grown up. *American Journal of Psychiatry, 151,* 670-674.

Lutzker, J. R., Bigelow, K. M., Doctor, R. M., Gershater, R. M., & Greene, B. F. (1998). An ecobehavioral model for the prevention and treatment of child abuse and neglect.

In J. R. Lutzker (Ed.), *Handbook of child abuse research and treatment* (pp. 239-266). New York: Plenum.

Maccoby, E. E. (1983). Social-emotional development and response to stressors. In N. Garmezy & M. Rutter (Eds.), *Stress, coping, and development in children* (pp. 217-234). New York: McGraw-Hill.

Maccoby, E. E., & Martin, J. A. (1983). Socialization in the context of the family: Parent-child interaction. In P. H. Mussen (Ed.), *Handbook of child psychology* (4th ed., pp. 1-101). New York: Wiley.

MacMillan, H. L., Fleming, J. E., Trocmé, N., Boyle, M. H., Wong, M., Racine, Y. A., Beardslee, W. R., & Offord, D. R. (1997). Prevalence of child physical and sexual abuse in the community: Results from the Ontario Health Supplement. *Journal of the American Medical Association, 278,* 131-135.

Main, M., & George, C. (1985). Responses of abused and disadvantaged toddlers to distress in agemates: A study in the daycare setting. *Developmental Psychology, 21,* 407-412.

Main, M., & Hesse, E. (1990). Parents' unresolved traumatic experiences are related to infant disorganized attachment status: Is frightened and/or frightening parental behavior the linking mechanism? In E. M. Greenberg, D. Cicchetti, & E. M. Cummings (Eds.), *Attachment in the preschool years* (pp. 161-182). Chicago: University of Chicago Press.

Main, M., & Solomon, J. (1990). Procedures for identifying infants as disorganized/disoriented during the Ainsworth Strange Situation. In M. Greenberg, D. Cicchetti, & E. M. Cummings (Eds.), *Attachment in the preschool years* (pp. 121-160). Chicago: University of Chicago Press.

Malamuth, N. M., Sockloskie, R. J., Koss, M. P., & Tanaka, J. S. (1991). Characteristics of aggressors against women: Testing a model using a national sample of college students. *Journal of Consulting and Clinical Psychology, 59,* 670-681.

Malinosky-Rummell, R., & Hansen, D. J. (1993). Long-term consequences of childhood physical abuse. *Psychological Bulletin, 114,* 68-79.

Mash, E. J., & Dozois, J. A. (1996). Child psychopathology: A developmental-systems perspective. In E. J. Mash & R. A. Barkley (Eds.), *Child psychopathology* (pp. 3-62). New York: Guilford.

Mash, E. J., Johnston, C., & Kovitz, K. (1983). A comparison of the mother-child interactions of physically abused and non-abused children during play and task situations. *Journal of Clinical Child Psychology, 12,* 337-346.

Masten, A. S., & Coatsworth, J. D. (1998). The development of competence in favorable and unfavorable environments: Lessons from research on successful children. *American Psychologist, 53,* 205-220.

Masten, A. S., & Garmezy, N. (1985). Risk, vulnerability, and protective factors in developmental psychopathology. In B. B. Lahey & A. E. Kazdin (Eds.), *Advances in clinical child psychology* (Vol. 8, pp. 1-52). New York: Plenum.

Maxfield, M. G., & Widom, C. S. (1996). The cycle of violence: Revisited 6 years later. *Archives of Pediatric and Adolescent Medicine, 150,* 390-395.

McCloskey, L., Figueredo, A., & Koss, M. (1995). The effects of systematic family violence on children's mental health. *Child Development, 66,* 1239-1261.

McCord, J. (1979). Some childrearing antecedents of criminal behavior in adult men. *Journal of Personality and Social Psychology, 37,* 1477-1486.

McCord, J. (1983). A forty year perspective on effects of child abuse and neglect. *Child Abuse & Neglect, 7,* 265-270.

McGee, R., & Wolfe, D. A. (1991). Psychological maltreatment: Towards an operational definition. *Development and Psychopathology, 3,* 3-18.

McLoyd, V. C. (1998). Socioeconomic disadvantage and child development. *American Psychologist, 53,* 185-204.

Melnick, B., & Hurley, J. R. (1969). Distinctive personality attributes of child-abusing mothers. *Journal of Consulting and Clinical Psychology, 33,* 746-749.

Melton, G. B. (1990). Child protection: Making a bad situation worse? *Contemporary Psychology, 35,* 213-214.

Melton, G. B., & Barry, F. D. (1994). Neighbors helping neighbors: The vision of the U.S. Advisory Board on Child Abuse and Neglect. In G. B. Melton & F. D. Barry (Eds.), *Protecting children from abuse and neglect: Foundations for a new national strategy* (pp. 1-13). New York: Guilford.

Merrill, E. J. (1962). Physical abuse of children: An agency study. In V. DeFrancis (Ed.), *Protecting the battered child.* Denver, CO: American Humane Association.

Merrill, L. L., Hervig, L. K., & Milner, J. S. (1996). Childhood parenting experience, intimate partner conflict resolution, and adult risk for child physical abuse. *Child Abuse & Neglect, 20,* 1049-1065.

Millstein, S. G., Petersen, A. C., & Nightingale, E. O. (1993). Adolescent health promotion: Rationale, goals, and objectives. In S. G. Millstein, A. C. Petersen, & E. O. Nightingale (Eds.), *Promoting the health of adolescents: New directions for the twenty-first century* (pp. 3-10). New York: Oxford University Press.

Milner, J. S. (1993). Social information processing and physical child abuse. *Clinical Psychology Review, 13,* 275-294.

Milner, J. S., & Wimberley, R. C. (1980). Prediction and explanation of child abuse. *Journal of Clinical Psychology, 36,* 875-884.

Morris, M., & Gould, R. (1963). Role reversal: A necessary concept in dealing with the battered child syndrome. *American Journal of Orthopsychiatry, 33,* 298-299.

Mullen, P. E., Martin, J. L., Anderson, J. C., Romans, S. E., & Herbison, G. P. (1996). The long-term impact of the physical, emotional, and sexual abuse of children: A community study. *Child Abuse & Neglect, 20,* 7-21.

Murphy, J. M., Jellinek, M., Quinn, D., Smith, G., Poitrast, F. G., & Goshko, M. (1991). Substance abuse and serious child mistreatment: Prevalence, risk, and outcome in a court sample. *Child Abuse & Neglect, 15,* 197-211.

National Research Council. (1993). *Understanding child abuse and neglect.* Washington, DC: National Academy Press.

Oldershaw, L., Walters, G. C., & Hall, D. K. (1986). Control strategies and noncompliance in abusive mother-child dyads: An observational study. *Child Development, 57,* 722-732.

Olds, D., Eckenrode, J., Henderson, C. R., Kitzman, H., Powers, J., Cole, R., Sidora, K., Morris, P., & Pettit, L. M. (1997). Long-term effects of home visitation on maternal life course and child abuse and neglect: Fifteen-year follow-up of a randomized trial. *Journal of the American Medical Association, 278*(8), 637-643.

Olds, D., Henderson, C., Chamberlin, R., & Tatelbaum, R. (1986). Preventing child abuse and neglect: A randomized trial of nurse home visitation. *Pediatrics, 78,* 65-78.

Olds, D., Henderson, C. R., & Kitzman, H. (1994). Does prenatal and infancy nurse home visitation have enduring effects on qualities of parental caregiving and child health at 25 to 50 months of life? *Pediatrics, 93,* 89-98.

Pamenter-Potvin, N. (1985). Physical abuse. In D. J. Besharov (Ed.), *Child abuse and neglect law: A Canadian perspective* (pp. 1-27). Washington, DC: Child Welfare League of America.

Parke, R. D. (1977). Socialization into child abuse: A social interactional perspective. In J. L. Tapp & F. J. Levine (Eds.), *Law, justice, and the individual in society: Psychological and legal issues* (pp. 183-199). New York: Holt, Rinehart & Winston.

Parke, R. D., & Collmer, C. W. (1975). Child abuse: An interdisciplinary analysis. In E. M. Hetherington (Ed.), *Review of child development research* (Vol. 5, pp. 509-590). Chicago: University of Chicago Press.

Parke, R. D., & Slaby, R. G. (1983). The development of aggression. In P. H. Mussen (Ed.), *Handbook of child psychology* (Vol. 4, pp. 547-641). New York: John Wiley.

Parker, J. G., & Herrera, C. (1996). Interpersonal processes in friendship: A comparison of abused and nonabused children's experiences. *Journal of Consulting and Clinical Psychology, 32,* 1023-1038.

Patterson, G. R. (1982). *Coercive family process.* Eugene, OR: Castalia.

Patterson, G. R., & Cobb, J. A. (1973). Stimulus control for classes of noxious behaviors. In J. Knutson (Ed.), *The control of aggression: Implications from basic research* (pp. 145-199). Chicago: Aldine.

Pelcovitz, D., Kaplan, S., Goldenberg, B., Mandel, F., Lehane, J., & Guarrera, J. (1994). Post-traumatic stress disorder in physically abused adolescents. *Journal of the American Academy of Child and Adolescent Psychiatry, 33,* 305-312.

Pelton, L. H. (1978). Child abuse and neglect: The myth of classlessness. *American Journal of Orthopsychiatry, 48,* 608-617.

Pelton, L. H. (1994). The role of material factors in child abuse and neglect. In G. B. Melton & F. D. Barry (Eds.), *Protecting children from abuse and neglect: Foundations for a new national strategy* (pp. 131-181). New York: Guilford.

Perez, C., & Widom, C. (1994). Childhood victimization and long-term intellectual and academic outcomes. *Child Abuse & Neglect, 18,* 617-633.

Peterson, L., & Brown, D. (1994). Integrating child injury and abuse-neglect research: Common histories, etiologies, and solutions. *Psychological Bulletin, 116,* 293-315.

Phares, V., & Compas, B. E. (1992). The role of fathers in child and adolescent psychopathology: Make room for Daddy. *Psychological Bulletin, 111,* 387-412.

Polansky, N. A., Gaudin, J. M., & Kilpatrick, A. C. (1992). Family radicals. *Children and Youth Services Review, 14,* 19-26.

Pollak, S. D., Cicchetti, D., Klorman, R., & Brumaghim, J. T. (1997). Cognitive brain event-related potentials and emotion processing in maltreated children. *Child Development, 68,* 773-787.

Radke-Yarrow, M., & Brown, E. (1993). Resilience and vulnerability in children of multiple-risk families. *Development and Psychopathology, 5,* 581-592.

Reid, J. B., Taplin, P., & Lorber, R. (1981). A social interactional approach to the treatment of abusive families. In R. B. Stuart (Ed.), *Violent behavior: Social learning approaches to prediction, management, and treatment* (pp. 83-101). New York: Brunner/Mazel.

Reidy, T. J. (1977). The aggressive characteristics of abused and neglected children. *Journal of Clinical Psychology, 33,* 1140-1145.

Rogosch, F. A., & Cicchetti, D. (1994). Illustrating the interface of peer and family relations through the study of child maltreatment. *Social Development, 3,* 291-308.

Rogosch, F. A., Cicchetti, D., & Aber, J. L. (1995). The role of child maltreatment in early deviations in cognitive and affective processing abilities and later peer relationship problems. *Development and Psychopathology, 7,* 591-609.

Rosenberg, M. S., & Reppucci, N. D. (1983). Abusive mothers: Perceptions of their own children's behavior. *Journal of Consulting and Clinical Psychology, 51,* 674-682.

Rosenberg, M. S., & Reppucci, N. D. (1985). Primary prevention of child abuse. *Journal of Consulting and Clinical Psychology, 53,* 576-585.

Rotenberg, K. J. (1980). Children's use of intentionality in judgments of character and disposition. *Child Development, 51,* 282-284.

Rutter, M. (1979). Protective factors in children's responses to stress and disadvantage. In M. W. Kent & J. E. Rolf (Eds.), *Primary prevention of psychopathology: Social competence in children* (pp. 49-74). Hanover, NH: University Press of New England (for the University of Vermont).

Rutter, M. (1983). Stress, coping, and development: Some issues and some questions. In N. Garmezy & M. Rutter (Eds.), *Stress, coping, and development in children* (pp. 1-41). New York: McGraw-Hill.

Salzinger, S., Feldman, R. S., Hammer, M., & Rosario, M. (1993). The effects of physical abuse on children's social relationships. *Child Development, 64,* 169-187.

Salzinger, S., Kaplan, S., & Artemyeff, C. (1983). Mothers' personal social networks and child maltreatment. *Journal of Abnormal Psychology, 92,* 68-76.

Salzinger, S., Kaplan, S., Pelcovitz, D., Samit, C., & Kreiger, R. (1984). Parent and teacher assessment of children's behavior in child maltreating families. *Journal of the American Academy of Child Psychiatry, 23,* 458-464.

Sameroff, A. J. (1993). Models of development and developmental risk. In C. H. Zeanah, Jr. (Ed.), *Handbook of infant mental health* (pp. 3-13). New York: Guilford.

Sameroff, A. J. (1995). General systems theories and developmental psychopathology. In D. Cicchetti & D. J. Cohen (Eds.), *Developmental psychopathology: Vol. 1. Theory and methods* (pp. 659-695). New York: John Wiley.

Sandgrund, A., Gaines, R. W., & Green, A. H. (1974). Child abuse and mental retardation: A problem of cause and effect. *Journal of Mental Deficiency, 79,* 327-330.

Scarr, S. (1992). Developmental theories for the 1990's: Development and individual differences. *Child Development, 63,* 1-19.

Scerbo, A. S., & Kolko, D. (1995). Child physical abuse and aggression: Preliminary findings on the role of internalizing problems. *Journal of the American Academy of Child and Adolescent Psychiatry, 34,* 1060-1066.

Schneider-Rosen, K., Braunwald, K., Carlson, V., & Cicchetti, D. (1985). Current perspectives in attachment theory: Illustration from the study of maltreated infants. In I. Bretherton & E. Waters (Eds.), *Growing points in attachment theory and research. Monographs of the Society for Research in Child Development, 50*(Serial No. 209), 194-210.

Schneider-Rosen, K., & Cicchetti, D. (1984). The relationship between affect and cognition in maltreated infants: Quality of attachment and the development of visual self-recognition. *Child Development, 55,* 648-658.

Schteingart, J. S., Molnar, J., Klein, T. P., Lowe, C. B., & Hartmann, A. H. (1995). Homelessness and child functioning in the context of risk and protective factors moderating child outcomes. *Journal of Clinical Child Psychology, 24,* 320-331.

Sedlak, A. J., & Broadhurst, D. D. (1996). *Third national incidence study of child abuse and neglect: Final report.* Washington, DC: U.S. Department of Health and Human Services.

Shantz, D. W., & Voyandoff, D. A. (1973). Situational effects on retaliatory aggression at three age levels. *Child Development, 44,* 149-153.

Shields, A. M., Cicchetti, D., & Ryan, R. M. (1994). The development of emotional and behavioral self-regulation and social competence among maltreated school-aged children. *Development and Psychopathology, 6,* 57-75.

Silverman, F. N. (1953). The roentgen manifestations of unrecognized skeletal trauma in infants. *American Journal of Reontgenology, 69,* 413-426.

Sipes, D. S. B. (1992). *Review of the literature on cultural considerations in treatment of abused and neglected ethnic minority children.* Paper prepared for the Working Group on Treatment of Child Abuse and Neglect, American Psychological Association, Washington, DC.

Smith, J. E. (1984). Non-accidental injury to children: 1. A review of behavioral interventions. *Behaviour Research and Therapy, 22,* 331-347.

Smith, S. M., Hanson, R., & Noble, S. (1974). Social aspects of the battered baby syndrome. *British Journal of Psychiatry, 125,* 568-582.

Spinetta, J. J. (1978). Parental personality factors in child abuse. *Journal of Consulting and Clinical Psychology, 46,* 1409-1414.

Spinetta, J. J., & Rigler, D. (1972). The child abusing parent: A psychological review. *Psychological Bulletin, 77,* 296-304.

Sroufe, L. A. (1989). Pathways to adaptation and maladaptation: Psychopathology as developmental deviation. In D. Cicchetti (Ed.), *Rochester Symposium on Developmental Psychopathology: Vol 1. The emergence of a discipline* (pp. 13-40). Hillsdale, NJ: Lawrence Erlbaum.

Sroufe, L. A., & Fleeson, J. (1986). Attachment and the construction of relationships. In W. Hartup & Z. Rubin (Eds.), *Relationships and development* (pp. 51-76). Hillsdale, NJ: Lawrence Erlbaum.

Sroufe, L. A., & Rutter, M. (1984). The domain of developmental psychopathology. *Child Development, 55,* 17-29.

Starr, R. H., Jr. (1982). A research-based approach to the prediction of child abuse. In R. H. Starr, Jr. (Ed.), *Child abuse prediction: Policy implications* (pp. 105-134). Cambridge, MA: Ballinger.

Statistics Canada. (1997). *People in low income* (Catalogue no. 13-207-XPB. Ottawa, ON: Author. Http://www.statcan.ca/english/Pgdb/People/Families/famil41.html

Steele, B. J., & Pollock, C. (1968). A psychiatric study of parents who abuse infants and small children. In R. Helfer & C. H. Kempe (Eds.), *The battered child* (pp. 89-133). Chicago: University of Chicago Press.

Steinberg, L., Lamborn, S. D., Darling, N., Mounts, N. S., & Dornbusch, S. M. (1994). Over-time changes in adjustment and competence among adolescents from authoritative, authoritarian, indulgent, and neglectful families. *Child Development, 65,* 754-770.

Straker, G., & Jacobson, R. S. (1981). Aggression, emotional maladjustment, and empathy in the abused child. *Developmental Psychology, 17,* 762-765.

Strassberg, Z. (1995). Social information processing in compliance situations by mothers of behavior-problem boys. *Child Development, 66,* 376-389.

Straus, M. A., & Donnelly, D. A. (1994). *Beating the devil out of them: Corporal punishment in American families.* New York: Lexington Books/Macmillan.

Straus, M. A., & Gelles, R. J. (1986). Societal change and change in family violence from 1975 to 1985 as revealed by two national surveys. *Journal of Marriage and the Family, 48,* 465-479.

Straus, M. A., & Gelles, R. J. (Eds.). (1990). *Physical violence in American families.* New Brunswick, NJ: Transaction Books.

Straus, M. A., Gelles, R. J., & Steinmetz, S. K. (1980). *Behind closed doors: Violence in the American family.* New York: Anchor.

Straus, M. A., & Kantor, G. K. (1994). Corporal punishment of adolescents by parents: A risk factor in the epidemiology of depression, suicide, alcohol abuse, child abuse, and wife beating. *Adolescence, 29,* 543-561.

Susman, E. J., Trickett, P. K., Iannotti, R. J., Hollenbeck, B. E., & Zahn-Waxler, C. (1985). Child-rearing patterns in depressed, abusive, and normal mothers. *American Journal of Orthopsychiatry, 55,* 237-251.

Tarter, R. E., Hegedus, A. E., Winsten, N. E., & Alterman, A. I. (1984). Neuropsychological, personality, and familial characteristics of physically abused delinquents. *Journal of the American Academy of Child Psychiatry, 23,* 668-674.

ten Bensel, R. W., Rheinberger, M. M., & Radbill, S. X. (1997). Children in a world of violence: The roots of child maltreatment. In M. E. Helfer, R. S. Kempe, & R. D. Krugman (Eds.), *The battered child* (5th ed., pp. 3-28). Chicago: University of Chicago Press.

Thompson, R. A. (1994). Social support and the prevention of child maltreatment. In G. B. Melton & F. D. Barry (Eds.), *Protecting children from abuse and neglect: Foundations for a new national strategy* (pp. 40-130). New York: Guilford.

Toth, S., Manly, J. T., & Cicchetti, D. (1992). Child maltreatment and vulnerability to depression. *Development and Psychopathology, 4,* 97-112.

Trickett, P. K., Aber, J. L., Carlson, V., & Cicchetti, D. (1991). The relationship of socioeconomic status to the etiology and development sequelae of physical child abuse. *Developmental Psychology, 27,* 148-158.

Trickett, P. K., & Kuczynski, L. (1986). Children's misbehaviors and parental discipline strategies in abusive and nonabusive families. *Developmental Psychology, 22,* 115-123.

Trocmé, N., McPhee, D., Tam, K. K., & Hay, T. (1994). *Ontario incidence study of reported child abuse and neglect.* Toronto: Institute for the Prevention of Child Abuse. (Available from the Institute for the Prevention of Child Abuse, 25 Spadina Ave., Toronto, Ont. M5R 2S9)

U.N. General Assembly. (1989). *Adoption of a convention on the rights of the child.* New York: Author.

U.S. Advisory Board on Child Abuse and Neglect. (1990). *Child abuse and neglect: Critical first steps in response to a national emergency.* Washington, DC: Government Printing Office.

U.S. Advisory Board on Child Abuse and Neglect. (1993). *Neighbors helping neighbors: A new national strategy for the protection of children.* Washington, DC: Government Printing Office.

Van der Kolk, B. A., & Fisler, R. E. (1994). Childhood abuse and neglect and loss of self-regulation. *Bulletin of the Menninger Clinic, 58,* 145-168.

Vasta, R. (1982). Physical child abuse: A dual component analysis. *Developmental Review, 2,* 164-170.

Vondra, J. A., Barnett, D., & Cicchetti, D. (1990). Self-concept, motivation, and competence among preschoolers from maltreating and comparison families. *Child Abuse & Neglect, 14,* 525-540.

Wallerstein, N. (1992). Powerlessness, empowerment, and health: Implications for health promotion programs. *American Journal of Health Promotion, 6* (3), 197-205.

Wasserman, S. (1967). The abused parent of the abused child. *Children, 14,* 175-179.

Wekerle, C., & Wall, A-M. (in press). The overlap between relationship violence and substance abuse. In C. Wekerle & A-M Wall (Eds.), *The violence and addiction equation: Theoretical and clinical issues in substance abuse and relationship violence.* Philadelphia: Brunner/Mazel.

Wekerle, C., & Wolfe, D. A. (1993). Prevention of child physical abuse and neglect: Promising new directions. *Clinical Psychology Review, 13,* 501-540.

Wekerle, C., & Wolfe, D. A. (1996). Child maltreatment. In E. J. Mash & R. A. Barkley (Eds.), *Child psychopathology* (pp. 492-537). New York: Guilford.

Whitmore, E. A. W., Kramer, J. R., & Knutson, J. F. (1993). The association between punitive childhood experiences and hyperactivity. *Child Abuse & Neglect, 17,* 357-366.

Widom, C. S. (1989a). The cycle of violence. *Science, 244,* 160-165.

Widom, C. S. (1989b). Does violence beget violence? A critical examination of the literature. *Psychological Bulletin, 106,* 3-28.

Widom, C. S. (1993). Child abuse and alcohol use and abuse. In S. E. Martin (Ed.), *Alcohol and interpersonal violence: Fostering interdisciplinary research* (NIAAA Research Monograph No. 24, NIH Publication No. 93-3496, pp. 291-314). Rockville, MD: National Institutes of Health.

Widom, C. (1998). Childhood victimization: Early adversity and subsequent psychopathology. In B. P. Dohrenwend (Ed.), *Adversity, stress, and psychopathology* (pp. 81-95). New York: Oxford University Press.

Williams, L. M. (1994). Recall of childhood trauma: A prospective study of women's memories of childhood sexual abuse. *Journal of Consulting and Clinical Psychology, 62,* 1167-1176.

Wolfe, D. A. (1985). Child abusive parents: An empirical review and analysis. *Psychological Bulletin, 97,* 462-482.

Wolfe, D. A. (1987). *Child abuse: Implications for child development and psychopathology.* Newbury Park, CA: Sage.

Wolfe, D. A. (1991). *Preventing physical and emotional abuse of children.* New York: Guilford.

Wolfe, D. A., Edwards, B., Manion, I., & Koverola, C. (1988). Early intervention for parents at-risk for child abuse and neglect: A preliminary investigation. *Journal of Consulting and Clinical Psychology, 56,* 40-47.

Wolfe, D. A., Fairbank, J., Kelly, J. A., & Bradlyn, A. S. (1983). Child abusive parents' physiological responses to stressful and nonstressful behavior in children. *Behavioral Assessment, 5,* 363-371.

Wolfe, D. A., & Jaffe, P. (1991). Child abuse and family violence as determinants of child psychopathology. *Canadian Journal of Behavioral Science, 23,* 282-299.

Wolfe, D. A., & Jaffee, P. (in press). Domestic violence prevention programs. *Futures of Children.*

Wolfe, D. A., Jaffe, P. J., Wilson, S. K., & Zak, L. (1985). Children of battered women: The relation of child behavior to family violence and maternal stress. *Journal of Consulting and Clinical Psychology, 53,* 657-665.

Wolfe, D. A., & MacEachran, A. (1997). Child abuse and neglect. In E. J. Mash & L. Terdal (Eds.), *Behavioral assessment of childhood disorders* (3rd ed., pp. 523-568). New York: Guilford.

Wolfe, D. A., & McGee, R. (1994). Dimensions of child maltreatment and their relationship to adolescent adjustment. *Development and Psychopathology, 6,* 165-181.

Wolfe, D. A., & Mosk, M. D. (1983). Behavioral comparisons of children from abusive and distressed families. *Journal of Consulting and Clinical Psychology, 51,* 702-708.

Wolfe, D. A., Sandler, J., & Kaufman, K. (1981). A competency-based parent training program for abusive parents. *Journal of Consulting and Clinical Psychology, 49,* 633-640.

Wolfe, D. A., Sas, L., & Wekerle, C. (1994). Factors associated with the development of posttraumatic stress disorder among child victims of sexual abuse. *Child Abuse & Neglect, 18,* 37-50.

Wolfe, D. A., & Wekerle, C. (1993). Treatment strategies for child physical abuse and neglect: A critical progress report. *Clinical Psychology Review, 13,* 473-500.

Wolfe, D. A., Wekerle, C., Reitzel-Jaffe, D., & Lefebvre, L. (1998). Factors associated with abusive relationships among maltreated and non-maltreated youth. *Development and Psychopathology, 10,* 61-85.

Wolfe, D. A., Wekerle, C., & Scott, K. (1997). *Alternatives to violence: Empowering youth to develop healthy relationships.* Thousand Oaks, CA: Sage.

Wolock, I., & Magura, S. (1996). Parental substance abuse as a predictor of child maltreatment re-reports. *Child Abuse & Neglect, 20,* 1183-1193.

World Health Organization. (1997, March). *Child abuse and neglect.* http://www.who.int/inf-fs/en/fact150.html

Wright, L. (1976). The "sick but slick" syndrome as a personality component of parents of battered children. *Journal of Clinical Psychology, 32,* 41-45.

Zahn-Waxler, C., Cole, P. M., Welsh, J. D., & Fox, N. A. (1995). Psychophysiological correlates of empathy and prosocial behaviors in preschool children with behavior problems. *Development and Psychopathology, 7,* 27-48.

Zillman, D. (1979). *Hostility and aggression.* Hillsdale, NJ: Lawrence Erlbaum.

AUTHOR INDEX

SUBJECT INDEX

Abused children. *See also specific headings*
 academic performance, 48
 age factors, 13-14
 and parental anger, 88-89
 attributions, 46-47
 compared to abusive parents, 46
 conduct problems, 49-50
 controlling behavior, 42
 cognitive and moral development, 45-48
 deficits in peer acceptance, 49
 deficits in social awareness, 45-46
 disabilities, 88
 empathy, 45
 gender factors, 14
 intellectual functioning, 48
 language development, 42
 peer relationships, 49-50
 self-control problems, 50
 social competence, 50-51
Abusive families:
 descriptive profile, 14-15
 interactions among members, 84-85
 isolation of, 90-91
 marital conflict among, 90
 observational studies of, 84-85
 power dynamics among, 85-86, 88
Abusive parents. *See also specific headings*
 child expectations and knowledge, 61, 64
 childhood experiences of, 57-58, 82-83, 85
 cognitive deficits and distortions, 84-85
 emotional arousal and reactivity, 86-87
 gender of, 15-16

 personality characteristics of, 57-65
 psychiatric disorders of, 86
Adaptational failure, 29
Adaptive functioning, 29
Affect:
 expression during parent-child interaction, 64
Aggression:
 among abused children, 49-51
 and misattributions, 47
 disinhibition of, 70-71
 in relation to child behavior, 89
 in relation to mood, 73-74
 mediating factors, 70
Alcohol abuse. *See* Substance abuse
Anger:
 and arousal, 64, 68, 86-87
 and parental attributions, 86
 early causes of, 87
 justification of, 74
 See also Treatment
Antisocial behavior, 53-55
Attachment:
 and child maltreatment, 40
 and development of social relations, 38
 insecure-disorganized, 41-42
 organized patterns of, 41
Attributions:
 of hostile intent, 47
Authoritarian parenting style
 and child development, 22-23
 definition of, 21-22

Battered child syndrome, 3

ABOUT THE AUTHOR

David A. Wolfe, Ph.D., is Professor of Psychology and Psychiatry at the University of Western Ontario in London, Canada. He is a founding member of the Center for Research on Violence Against Women and Children at the University and past President of Division 37 (Child, Youth, and Family Services) of the American Psychological Association. He has broad research and clinical interests in abnormal child psychology, with a special focus on child abuse, domestic violence, and developmental psychopathology. He has authored numerous articles on these topics, especially in relation to the impact of early childhood trauma on later development in childhood, adolescence, and early adulthood. Recent books include *Children of Battered Women,* with P. Jaffe and S. Wilson (1990); *Preventing Physical and Emotional Abuse of Children* (1991); *Alternatives to Violence: Empowering Youth to Develop Healthy Relationships,* with C. Wekerle and K. Scott (1996); and *Abnormal Child Psychology,* with E. Mash (1999).

Made in the USA
Middletown, DE
05 September 2015